THE PSYCHOLO

How do some political leaders capture popular support? What is the appeal of belonging to a nation? Can democracy thrive?

The Psychology of Politics explores how the emotions which underpin everyday life are also vital in what happens on the political stage. It draws on psychoanalytic ideas to show how fear and passion shape the political sphere in our changing societies and cultures, and examines topical social issues and events including Brexit, the changing nature of democracy, activism, and Trump in America.

In a changing global political climate, *The Psychology of Politics* shows us how we can make sense of what drives human conduct in relation to political ideas and action.

Barry Richards is Professor of Political Psychology in the Faculty of Media and Communication at Bournemouth University.

THE PSYCHOLOGY OF EVERYTHING

People are fascinated by psychology, and what makes humans tick. Why do we think and behave the way we do? We've all met armchair psychologists claiming to have the answers, and people that ask if psychologists can tell what they're thinking. *The Psychology of Everything* is a series of books which debunk the popular myths and pseudo-science surrounding some of life's biggest questions.

The series explores the hidden psychological factors that drive us, from our subconscious desires and aversions, to our natural social instincts. Absorbing, informative, and always intriguing, each book is written by an expert in the field, examining how research-based knowledge compares with popular wisdom, and showing how psychology can truly enrich our understanding of modern life.

Applying a psychological lens to an array of topics and contemporary concerns – from sex, to fashion, to conspiracy theories – *The Psychology of Everything* will make you look at everything in a new way.

Titles in the series:

For further information about this series please visit www.thepsychologyofeverything.co.uk

THE
PSYCHOLOGY
OF POLITICS

BARRY RICHARDS

Routledge
Taylor & Francis Group

LONDON AND NEW YORK

First published 2019
by Routledge
2 Park Square, Milton Park, Abingdon, Oxon OX14 4RN

and by Routledge
52 Vanderbilt Avenue, New York, NY 10017

Routledge is an imprint of the Taylor & Francis Group, an informa business

British Library Cataloguing-in-Publication Data
A catalogue record for this book is available from the British Library

Library of Congress Cataloging-in-Publication Data
A catalog record has been requested for this book

ISBN: 978-1-138-55167-1 (hbk)
ISBN: 978-1-138-55170-1 (pbk)
ISBN: 978-1-315-14769-7 (ebk)

Typeset in Joanna
by Apex CoVantage, LLC
Printed by CPI Group (UK) Ltd, Croydon CR0 4YY

CONTENTS

1

THE HEART OF POLITICS

The heart has its reasons, of which reason knows nothing.

(Blaise Pascal, *Thoughts*, 1670)

OUR PSYCHOLOGICAL ERA

By the end of the last century, it had become clear that, in many countries around the world, we were living in a psychological era. Psychology had become one of the most popular subject choices amongst university students, and it had become normal in many theatres of everyday life to take an interest in psychological issues. What is this person feeling? Why is that person behaving like that? How are we affected by different sorts of experience? Can people really change themselves? Not everyone thinks that the trend towards asking such questions is a good thing, and indeed it is not always done in good ways. We will touch on some of the current debates later in the book. But overall, there are many reasons to welcome this major shift in our culture, which we can see as laying the basis for growth in our collective reserves of self-understanding, sensitivity, resilience and − above all − concern for others. We will use the term *emotional capital* to refer to these shared assets, which are of great importance to the future of our societies.

Yet despite the growing influence of psychology in education, in some professions and in popular culture, it has had little impact on politics – on how we understand politics, let alone on political practices. The turn to psychology is happening differently in different areas of life. It happened very quickly in some areas of popular culture, where there were pre-existing preoccupations with romantic love and family life. In politics, however, we may readily assume that economic interests and military strength are the ultimate forces at work, and that they leave little room for our psychologies to influence events. Also, amongst academics and other intellectuals, the desire to hold on to un-psychological explanations of human behaviour has been particularly strong when it comes to politics.

Take, for example, the idea that our voting choices are primarily based on the state of the economy, and so are determined by our calculations of which party or candidate would be best for our individual economic self-interest: 'Under which party would I be best off?' This model of the citizen as a rational *homo economicus* may sometimes capture one element in the mix of factors determining some people's electoral decisions, but it is of no use as a theory of how democracy works psychologically.[1] Other broader models of the individual, which weigh up more complex issues than economic self-interest, may still rely on an underlying conception of the citizen as a fundamentally rational agent, untroubled by any tumult of feeling. This rationalistic approach cannot dig deeper into the emotions which are often fundamental to voting choices, and to other political behaviours, and which need to be understood psychologically. Despite the growing interest in emotion across the social sciences in recent decades, the continuing influence of the old philosophical tradition of rationalism has slowed the development of a fully psychological approach to understanding politics, inside and outside academia. We remain impressed by the certainty of 'It's the economy, stupid'.

One reason for this is the disturbing uncertainty of where we might end up if we were to open the door of politics to psychology – to open it so fully that we might then see the ostensibly hard-headed business of politics as a maelstrom of passion and fear. The hyper-rationalist self needs to feel that it knows itself, and a psychology which challenges the claim to self-knowledge will probably be unwelcome, especially if it focusses on the more difficult aspects of human nature. This book argues that there are reasons to be more optimistic about human nature than many people are at present, but also that there are destructive forces in our internal worlds which our societies often do not manage well, and which in fact they often amplify.

We also discuss how a psychological understanding of politics must get away from any idea that there is a clear separation between mental health and mental malaise. There are sensitivities today around using the diagnostic terms of psychiatry, and the general language of psychopathology, to refer to conditions of distress and dysfunction, since such language is held by its critics to stigmatise the people to whom it is applied, and to medicalise what are actually 'problems in living',[2] usually with social causes. The whole field of mental health is still bedevilled by its capture by medicine in the nineteenth century. Notwithstanding the excellent work that many psychiatric professionals do in supporting and caring for people with mental health difficulties, the basic idea that mental health problems can be seen as equivalent to physical illnesses is seriously unhelpful. What psychiatric language suggests are discrete disease entities or structural deformities of the mind (e.g. 'paranoid psychosis' or 'borderline personality disorder') are actually the consequences in an individual of the complex psychosocial processes that constitute living in a society.

However, while it is absolutely right and necessary to stress the basic continuity and sameness between those described as 'mentally ill' and those who are officially not 'ill', this does not mean that psychopathology is a fiction. Disturbed and perverse states of mind do exist, and they bring damage to individuals and to society. The important point for our purposes here is to note that when we have to use terms such as 'narcissistic', 'psychotic' and so on (which we do across many areas of political psychology), we are not trying to explain something by seeing it as the result of a disease from which some people suffer, and others don't. We can *explain* what individual people say or do (whether they are ordinary citizens or national leaders) only by studying the particular lives they have lived in their contexts. But we can *describe* the psychological qualities of what we all say or do by using some of the terminology of psychopathology, as long as we remember that the processes and states of mind we refer to are found in all of us, as part of our make-up, and are not alien diseases.

Political psychology should have no hesitation in stating that pathological states of mind can be mobilised in any of us, and that mental health is therefore a political issue in the widest sense – not as an area of policy that demands higher priority (though it is that), but as something which is constitutive of the public and of society, and therefore of politics. Actually, our collective mental health (our emotional capital) is likely to determine the future of democracy.

Fortunately, a spirit of psychological enquiry is now growing in relation to politics, partly owing to the continued spread of psychological awareness, but unfortunately also to adverse developments on the world stage. We are now seeing a number of major phenomena which clearly demand an understanding of their roots in the emotional and irrational dimensions of human conduct. Some of these are new, for example, the rise of global terrorism, and the de-stabilisation of hitherto stable liberal democracies; others are re-emerging, or being noticed more clearly, such as the proliferation of crudely authoritarian regimes, and the damaging effects of poorly regulated markets. The influence of the destructive, often self-destructive, sides of human nature is now calling for our attention, whether we are specialist students of politics or ordinary people trying to make a bit more sense of the world in order to be less blind in our role as citizens, and to see a little more of the prospects facing coming generations.

The psychology of politics is a growing specialism in academia, and could be on the threshold of a step-change in the scope and influence of its contributions to political discourse. This short book is an attempt to formulate an approach to understanding the psychology of politics which focusses on the emotional and unconscious drivers of human conduct. In doing so, it draws heavily on ideas from the psychoanalytic tradition, which more than any other school of thought has tried to confront and understand the sources of destructiveness.

But this does not take us entirely into a world of darkness, because in looking deeply into the psyche we will also encounter the deep roots of the capacities for empathy, concern and generosity. And those positive capacities are as emotional and as 'irrational' (at least in a narrow sense of 'rationality') as are the impulses towards destruction. So, as the seventeenth-century French philosopher Blaise Pascal had suggested in the now often-quoted line from his posthumous work 'Thoughts', we need to come out of the falsely dichotomised world of early modern philosophy in which rationality, intellect and progress stand on one side, with irrationality, emotion and backwardness on the other. Psychoanalysis transcends that dichotomy, and it enables us to see that the question is not whether reason or emotion is the driver, since both are always involved, but what kinds of emotion are involved, and therefore to which purposes reason is put.

THINKING PSYCHOSOCIALLY

The psychology of politics is basically the same as the psychology of anything else. Our experiences and actions in the political domain are shaped by the same fundamental emotional needs and resources as we find at the centre of our personal lives, and in our work and leisure activities. Political psychology is therefore the study of how these basic forces play out in the context of politics. In different contexts, different parts of our selves come more into play, which is why psychological inquiry should always be linked with a study of the social context – the fundamental principle of psychosocial analysis, which this book will hopefully illustrate. In political contexts, whether we are voters, activists, leaders, or ordinary people just trying to decide what we think and feel about the news, it is our selves as members of wider communities which will be in the foreground. And these 'citizen' types of self may differ in some ways from one's self as friend, partner, parent, sibling, colleague and so on. Still, all our selves are rooted in the psychological fundamentals which we all share.

In the approach to be taken throughout this book, these fundamentals will be seen as *needs* and *resources* – emotional needs for certain kinds of experience and certain kinds of relationship, and emotional resources for meeting life's demands. This approach is based primarily on contemporary psychoanalysis and its understanding of psychological development. Not all psychologists would take this approach, because psychology is not a unified discipline. Its different schools of thought can differ quite radically on important issues. The popular idea that psychology is a 'science' may hide this disunity from public view. We know that scientists within a discipline may argue, but we expect them to speak the same broad language. Yet psychology is actually a profusion of different languages.

Some academics in the field of 'political psychology' would not regard this book as part of that field, because it does not speak in the language of evidence that they use, which typically is a language of *quantitative* analysis – of measuring aspects of our psychological lives in numerical terms, and using statistical analyses of those numbers to try and figure out what is going on in our minds. There are many critiques of that approach, on the grounds that it too often seems to come up with fairly obvious conclusions which we might have reached anyway, and that it is rarely able to capture the depth and complexity of our emotional and social lives. There are also critiques of the *qualitative* approach to be taken here, with its psychoanalytic focus on exploring states of mind using a theory of the unconscious, and of how our minds develop and function under the influence of unconscious processes. For some psychologists this is too reliant on how the researcher chooses to interpret the words and actions of the people under study.

It is not the purpose of this book to examine those debates, though they are important. The aim here is to set out the basics of a psychosocial and psychoanalytic approach to understanding the psychological dimensions of politics. Even within the psychoanalytic tradition, there are different views of what the key ideas are. The ones I offer have a broad base in contemporary psychoanalytic thinking, in the particular tradition of what is called 'object relations' theory. This may seem an odd name, since this approach is very much about us as persons not as 'objects' in the common sense of the word. The reason for this phrase will become clear a little later in this chapter.

THE SAFETY PRINCIPLE

Our starting point is the proposition that there are two fundamental needs which underlie all our psychologies: a need for safety and a need for dignity. These needs lie at the heart of politics. The importance of the experience of safety is central to the tradition of thinking about psychological development known as attachment theory, an offshoot of psychoanalysis initiated by the psychoanalyst John Bowlby in the 1940s. His theory begins with the biological phenomenon of hard-wired attachments between parents and infants in all mammalian species, which normally ensures that the parents are attentive to the young and that offspring stay close to parents. This is necessary for species-preservation, given the helplessness and vulnerability of the young. Possession of a 'secure base' is also crucial for psychological development in humans, as it gives a platform for exploration on which a capacity for independence can be built.

Bowlby (1988) observed that in human infants this built-in need for attachment is not always adequately met by the infant's caregivers, with the result that a feeling of safety is not securely achieved. He described several patterns of 'insecure attachment' which could result, seen in different emotional and behavioural difficulties. These are likely to leave their mark in the formation of adult personality. Insecurities are therefore handed down the generations, as those with a weaker inner belief in a secure base are less likely to be able to create a sense of safety for their own children.

The sense of safety depends on trust in the environment – specifically in the adult(s) who are the superpowers in the infant's environment. The centrality of trust in the first months of psychological development was made clear by psychoanalyst Erik Erikson, who was one of the originators of psychosocial thinking. In his book *Childhood and Society*, first published in 1950, he saw resolving the 'conflict of basic trust versus basic mistrust' as the 'first task' facing the baby and its caregiver. He suggested that religions, with their faith in a benign power, are institutional expressions of basic trust – though of course they can also be seen as illusions of a trustworthy universe which does not exist. Much more could be said about this, but for our purposes here the point is that a measure of trust in its environment is necessary for the infant to develop psychologically in a good-enough way. Because of its total dependency on others, it must be able to trust that others will meet its needs. Without that trust, it would be continually exposed to panic and terror at the awareness of its own helplessness.

The psychoanalyst Joseph Sandler (1987) suggested that the primary principle governing mental life was the 'safety principle', according to which securing an experience of safety is our overriding objective. This is not the same as a 'survival instinct' with the simple goal of physical safety, though it may include that. We are psychological creatures, so the safety we need is a mental one, a *feeling* safe. The most fundamental type of this kind of safety is feeling safe in one's own mind. That may seem like an odd suggestion: how could you not be 'safe' just in your own mind? The answer is to be found in the sufferings of mental disorder: the fears and panics of neurotic anxiety, the feelings of internal deadness in depression, and the terrifying experiences of disintegration in psychotic states of mind, show that we cannot take the stability or integrity of our own minds for granted.

Psychoanalytic investigation of early psychological development has suggested that our earliest experience as babies, before our selves have achieved a substantial degree of integration, can easily be dominated by a fear of falling apart, of annihilation. The best antidote to such fear is the experience of being 'recognised' by another person, that is of having your fears acknowledged, and your self affirmed and accepted, by another. The provision of such experiences for the human infant naturally falls to the infant's main carer(s). A leading figure in post-Freudian psychoanalysis, Donald Winnicott, wrote extensively in the mid-twentieth century about the role of the 'ordinary, good-enough' mother in attuning to her baby's needs and fears, from the mild to the overwhelming, and so facilitating the development in the infant's mind of a stable sense of self inhabiting a reasonably supportive environment (see, for example, Winnicott, 1988). Thus a basis is laid for the experience and the expectation of safety. The work of the mother, and other primary care-givers, in helping to create this vital sense of safety, was captured in Winnicott's concept of 'holding'. In part this is a physical holding, in an attentive and empathic way that enables an infant to feel safe in the external world and in its own body, but it is more than that — Winnicott talks of the 'holding environment'.

Yet no caregivers, however loving and attuned, can provide perfect and instant administration to the baby's needs. No matter how devoted the parent, there will be distracting demands on their attention, delays in feeding or changing, interruptions and separations. There will be pain and frustration. So there will be recurrent occasions for feeling unsafe, for doubting that the world is trustworthy. One of the major projects of psychoanalysis has been to explore this area of development and its legacies in the adult mind. Insofar as a basic sense of safety was established in infancy, this will be a resource that can contribute to emotional well-being throughout life. But while the experience of safety remains brittle or weak, or access to it is unreliable, the individual may be vulnerable, or dysfunctional, perhaps at risk of exploitation or manipulation by various promises of safety.

The connection here with politics is clear, especially in times when even citizens of stable and lawful democracies have reason to feel unsafe. So when political leaders strive to win the trust of the people, they are entering territory where powerful and complex forces are at work. Adult voters, trying to decide whom to trust, are judging what they think they can see of the candidates, but are also unknowingly comparing the candidates with their own buried memories or hopes about what trustworthiness looks, sounds or feels like. We will explore more of that later, but here we must stay for a little while longer in this territory of difficult psychological theory, to meet some more of the ideas which will be applied in subsequent chapters.

SPLIT WORLDS

There has been much psychoanalytic investigation of how infants and young children deal with feeling unsafe, which has partly built on, and partly transformed, the foundations which the first psychoanalyst Sigmund Freud laid for understanding the mind. This work has produced a number of concepts describing the defences which we employ in our minds to try to obliterate the unsafety, and so avoid the anxiety associated with it. The most basic of these is the process of *splitting*, in which all the objects of our experience (of which people are of course the most important) are divided into two categories, the absolutely 'good' and the absolutely 'bad'. These dramatically split objects of experience in the baby's mind exemplify what psychoanalysts call 'unconscious phantasies' – hidden internal templates which shape our experience of the external world, and determine its meaning for us. The rudimentary way of making sense of the world by splitting it may to some extent be a spontaneous feature of the infant mind – good = warm, satisfied, held, etc., while bad = cold, hungry, alone, etc. Perhaps the polarity of good/bad is its only way of ordering experience until it develops cognitively and is able to make other and more complex discriminations.

But the lasting significance of splitting is in its power as an *active* defence. It enables the infant – and later the adult – to find an object of its experience which is entirely good, something in which it can trust and in relation to which it therefore feels safe. Typically, this is an image of the mother or primary caregiver, comprising only positive elements of the infant's experience of her. Those other sensations and impressions of her which are associated with unsafety (via negative experiences of pain, frustration or anxiety) are organised into a separate object, the source of bad experience. In this way, our inner world is structured by ambivalence. Our early experience of the one reality outside us is split into two, so there is a good object, which is loved, and a bad one, which is feared and hated. Both are phantasies, though linked to elements of reality. Over time, this duality of an idealised, perfect object and a denigrated, bad one will be broken down by the cumulative effects of exposure to reality, by experiences which demonstrate that there is actually just one person out there who is the source of both types of experience. However, that achievement depends on the infant having developed enough trust in the goodness of the mother to be able to continue to trust her when she is no longer experienced in a split, idealised way. If the 'integrated object' is not experienced as fundamentally good and trustworthy, it cannot be fully trusted, and so there will be a tendency to revert to splitting and to seek safety in an idealised object.[3]

This may be as true of the adult as it is of the baby and young child. We will be coming across many examples in politics of the influence of split views of the world. The developmental shift to more integrated perceptions occurs through the early years of development in infancy and childhood, but is never complete and permanent. Even when, as adults, we may feel we have become fully aware of the complexity of the world, we can at an unconscious level be pulled towards the safety to be found in the simplifications of splitting and the starkly ambivalent, 'schizoid' state of mind it produces.

The development of the concept of the early, primitive defence of splitting is one of the contributions of the Kleinian tradition in psychoanalysis, based on the mid-twentieth century work in London of the psychoanalyst Melanie Klein. A distinctive contribution of this school is the emphasis it places on the destructive tendency in human nature, which it sees as intrinsic to our make-up and not as something which appears only in response to bad experience. In this connection, Kleinians see splitting as typically operating in conjunction with another defence, one which Freud identified but which has been much elaborated in post-Freudian theory: the defence of *projection*. This is the process whereby we imagine that some aspect of ourselves which we find intolerable does not actually belong in our internal world, but exists in somebody (or something) in the external world. We project this quality out, onto some external object. Thus an aggressive or destructive impulse felt to be in the self can be projected outwards and experienced as being lodged out there, where it is then felt to be a threat. This process is the basis of the phobias, in which something in the external world becomes the focus of irrational fear, and of states of mind we call paranoid, in which there is felt to be an active threat to the self from outside itself. In both cases the threat is actually within, and so projection is necessary to preserve an experience of the individual's mind as a safe place.[4] We may also project outwards the idealised parts of the self, when we need to create for ourselves an experience of someone in the external world as ideal (as we may with a lover, or a leader).

Another major defence against terrifying unsafety, one which we will frequently encounter in following chapters, is that of *narcissism*. This is best pictured as a composite defence, resting on specific variations of splitting and projection. The splitting involved is not between the good and bad elements of experience of objects that exist outside the self (such as good and bad mothers, good and bad leaders or political parties), but between self and other, such that the self is idealised while all negative qualities are located outside the self, having been placed there by the evacuative work of projection. The purpose of this is to experience the self as sufficient unto itself, and therefore as invulnerable to the terrors of dependency on an untrustworthy other. This idealisation of the self is a far more complex and deceptive phenomenon than the popular idea of narcissism as vanity and egotistical self-regard. For example, narcissism as an unconscious mindset can underlie an exterior personality which is apparently self-deprecating and interested in other people. The narcissistic refusal to acknowledge any need for others may be buried quite deeply in the personality.

THE DIGNITY PRINCIPLE

This principle holds that another predominant psychological need is for an experience of dignity. Psychoanalysis has had less to say directly about dignity than about safety, and surprisingly nor has psychology as a whole focussed much on this important dimension of human experience, with the exception of the work of Evelin Lindner (2006) and others on dignity and humiliation. Dignity and the related concepts of respect and esteem have been discussed more in the social sciences than in psychology, as in the works of the sociologist Richard Sennett on 'respect' (2003), the sociologist and political scientist Liah Greenfeld on dignity (as we will see in Chapter 3), and the philosophers Axel Honneth on 'recognition' (1995) and Avishai Margalit (1996) on 'decency'. Margalit argues that a decent society is one which does not humiliate any of its members. What follows is a brief summary of a psychosocial view of dignity, drawing on the same psychoanalytic perspective we used to consider safety.

While the need for safety can be linked to a universal, genetically coded imperative (albeit one that culture extends and refashions in complex ways), the need for dignity may be more generated by socio-historical forces. In the very broad context of modern society, where 'modern' means all those societies in which the forces of democracy and liberalism have shaped fundamental beliefs about what and who we are, some notion of the free and responsible individual has become a defining criterion of a good enough life. Consequently the need for individuals to feel that they have some autonomy and personal dignity in the world has sunk deeply into their psyches. In societies with more collectivistic traditions, dignity may be more defined by acceptance within the group, although the influence of 'Western' individualism seems to be increasingly global.

While the need for a sense of dignity, and the pain at its absence, may be embedded in the societal context, when considered as an element of psychological development it can be seen as an expression of the universal need to be loved. Comfortably sustaining the experience of dignity is difficult without some external confirmation, but the capacity to feel a sense of dignity is fundamentally one of *self*-respect, which in turn is built on an experience of the self as being of value, and worthy of love. This is closely tied, like the safety principle, to our starting situation of dependence. The situation of total dependence on others is a threatening one, not only because physical survival may be at stake but because it is one of helplessness in the face of others' power. What prevents this early experience from being one of scarring fear and humiliation is the infant's experience of being loved, and its creation from that of a core sense of itself as worthy of love. So we arrive again at the emotional content of the earliest caring relationships, and the development of trust – in the caring other, and in the lovability value of the emerging self.

Under that influence, the humiliation of dependency can be accepted, and emotional development can proceed without the baggage of resentment or rage, and with a sense of being valued by another, which is the platform for the sense of dignity. Paradoxically, then, the acceptance of humiliation leads to a capacity for dignity.

In situations of reduced or absent trust, dependency is difficult to experience as a tolerable condition, especially when the trust deficit has led to the development of a narcissistic defence, under which any acknowledgment, let alone toleration, of humiliating dependency is impossible. It is therefore not surprising that we find many examples (particularly in war and terrorism, as well as in some apolitical crime) of actions driven by a sense of intolerable humiliation. There are also many social contexts in which parenting practices throughout childhood can add a surplus of humiliation to the normal experience of growing up. Parenting which is coloured by domineering or contemptuous ways of relating to the child, or which instils a sense of shame about bodily functions or sexuality, may complicate or sabotage the task of developing dignity.

INSIDE AND OUTSIDE: THE IDENTITY BRIDGE

Many complications also beset the processes by which the capacity to experience safety and dignity becomes established, and is then either strengthened or eroded in later development and adult life. A psychosocial approach would try to distinguish between 'internal' and 'external' factors determining the levels of both safety and dignity in particular situations. External factors are those present in the current environment, while internal factors are those brought to the situation in the minds of the people under consideration – many of which may be the product of earlier external forces. For example, a group unhappy with its lot as a minority within a nation governed by members of the majority group may feel both unsafe and lacking dignity. A major external factor would be the extent to which the government is actually threatening it or discriminating against it. Internal factors might include a precarious sense of safety, or low standing levels of personal dignity, such that some members of the group had low thresholds for believing themselves to be threatened or excluded. This might be the result of historical experience of threats or exclusion (possibly even affecting the previous generation), or of other factors more related to the culture of the minority group (e.g. authoritarian family structures). Of course, the presence of internal factors does not reduce the need for the external ones to change.

One concept which bridges between internal and external is that of identity, which is increasingly important in political analysis not only because of the rise of 'identity politics' but also because of its use in psychosocial inquiry, as a link between inside and outside, between who I feel I am and the social forces which have shaped me. The concept began with Erik Erikson, for whom it was the confident possession of a sense of inner coherence and continuity, acquired in adolescence when the developing self seeks to locate itself in wider society. Identity also links safety and dignity, since people seek dignity in their social and cultural identities, while also finding some psychological safety in the social belonging which an identity implies.

'Identity' is therefore a rich psychosocial concept which we can use to examine both psychological and societal processes and how they infuse each other. It also denotes a force in modern society which is both very positive and potentially very destructive. Our predominant associations to the term tend to be positive; in Erikson's initial formulations, a strong identity is the precious acquisition of an individual developmental process that has gone well. It implies a sense of meaning in life, and of integration into society. It is the mark of secure individual selfhood. A coherent and meaningful sense of personal identity is psychologically, and therefore societally, beneficial.

An important component of personal identity is derived from the large social groups to which we belong and with which we identify – the identifications we make with region or nation, religion or class, political or lifestyle 'tribe'. The Turkish-American psychoanalyst Vamik Volkan, whose work (e.g. 2004) is foundational to the approach taken in this book, argues that large group identity is a vital component of the self – it is what he calls a *core identity*, which means that its stability is of importance to the individual's sense of well-being, even though it is usually in the background of self-experience. The most important large group identity for many people is national identity, though active awareness of that is not a major feature of everyday life for most people. Yet in his analyses of various national identities, Volkan focusses more – inevitably perhaps given that his specialism has been the understanding and resolution of conflict – on the regressive potential of these large group identifications, and their role in the creation and maintenance of conflicts. And generally, when social scientists have turned to look at *collective* identities, they have often found them to be at best mixed in their consequences. One of Volkan's many contributions has been to show how large group identities become problematic when they are constructed or deployed *defensively*, as a way of maintaining a sense of safety and/or dignity in response to a crisis, loss or threat of some kind.

As well as its role in violent conflicts, the idea and the experience of collective identity has functioned to support divisive and fragmenting political trends in recent years. While this is a complex area, and benefits have come from 'identity politics' in the basic voice and dignities it has brought to social groups which were hitherto effectively excluded from the public sphere, a constant focus on sectional identities and interests can have a corrosive effect on democratic culture. If a self-selected 'identity' is enough to merit a platform and proclaim an agenda, then anyone can pile in and make demands. There is also a telling irony in the way that the 'identitarian' movement of various 'alt-right' and anti-Islam groups in present-day Europe and the US appears to have named itself after one of the signature concepts of the 1968 generation of radicals, whose legacy of liberalism it sees as deeply damaging and seeks to overturn.

The key point psychologically, however, is that defensive mobilisations of large group identity (in which aggression is often the chosen means of defence) do not arise spontaneously. They are the result of threats to that identity, whether very real at political and material levels, or very real in the shared phantasy life of the group.

In some cases, depending on the nature of the perceived threats, the safety-related themes of territory and security may be the priority; in others, it could be a dignity agenda of rights and equality which is most prominent.

THE PSYCHO-CULTURAL CONTEXT AND EMOTIONAL CAPITAL

It may be evident now what the emotional resources mentioned at the start of this chapter are. Most of the discussion above has been about the needs for safety and dignity, and the problems which arise when those needs are not met. But it has implied that when they are adequately met, especially in the course of early emotional development, powerful emotional resources are created: individuals acquire a strong internal sense of safety and reserves of confident dignity. And there is a further, vital resource which is built on these and which once established also acts to enhance the well-being of others, which is the capacity held by individuals across a society to contain difficult emotions, both in themselves and in others. We have partly introduced this earlier, with reference to the concept of 'holding' used by Donald Winnicott, but it is worth spelling it out more fully.

The capacity for *containment* is an important concept in psychotherapeutic work and in the understanding of the relationships between individuals and the organisations, communities and societies of which they are a part. It refers to the process by which difficult feelings such as anxiety, guilt, loss and anger can be managed most constructively for the individual concerned, and for others with whom that person may be in contact. The feeling has to be acknowledged rather than defensively denied or disowned, and it has to be tolerated without recourse to any action or psychological manoeuvre which would distract from or obliterate it. We learn this capacity for emotional self-management very early in life, from the ways in which the caregiver conveys an empathic recognition and soothing toleration of the baby's distress and anger. Anxious, depressed or distracted parents may have trouble doing this well enough. Feelings which cannot be faced and contained must then be dealt with using one of the defence mechanisms which psychoanalysis has studied, two of which have been mentioned above (splitting and projection), and others of which will be described later. Defences are maladaptive and generate problems both in an individual's personal life and, when we deploy them collectively, at organisational and societal levels.

These psychological resources of safety, dignity and containment can be seen as the bases of the 'emotional capital' available in any given society or community. The depth of these resources in a society will depend on how much the adult individuals in that society are in possession of them, which in turn will depend primarily on what kind of growing up they experienced, how much it left them able to feel safe, self-respecting and strong. A considerable burden in trying to sustain emotional capital falls on the caring and therapeutic professions who are charged with dealing with and trying to remedy the consequences of damaged psychological development.[5] Still, the main factor will be how well the psycho-cultural make-up of a society facilitates good emotional development, i.e. how the patterns of family life, social relationships and everyday behaviours impact upon the child's development. In particular there is what we might call a 'parental matrix', comprising the cluster of primary caregivers (the one, two or more people providing the main childcare, whether or not they are actual parents) and their personalities, how they relate to the baby/child, the situations of care, and the child's experience of it all. This matrix shapes what kind of people we are, how we experience the world and feel about it, and therefore what levels of emotional capital we can contribute to our society. Of course, societies are not homogeneous in this regard; there are huge variations in emotional capital between families, let alone between different social and cultural groups. But the overall levels of societal provision for well-being, and cultural traditions, will affect every individual for better or worse.

A society's emotional resources will be especially called upon when it is under stress or threat, as when a nation is in conflict with another nation, or internally. Our emotional capital will influence what kinds of outcome to a conflict we are able to imagine and to accept. The basics of an in-depth psychological approach to violent conflict can be described in relatively simple terms. It involves three foci of exploration: how involvement in the conflict is an attempt by its protagonists to meet their basic psychological needs for safety and dignity; why these needs were not being met in more constructive ways; and how they might be met in a process of negotiation and conflict resolution. This basic approach is of equal relevance to understanding many forms of political violence, from urban riots and local wars of secession to genocides and large-scale regional conflicts.

It will be of more importance in some situations than others, depending on factors such as how protracted the conflict has been (and how much it has thereby sunk into the psyches of the peoples involved), how central it is to the identities of the antagonists, and how pressing the non-psychological issues are: is the existence of a group at risk, will the outcome of the conflict have quick and major impact on the health or safety of a community, or determine its long-term wealth and welfare, and so on. Some 'conflict' situations may be better called situations of 'infliction', because there has been stark oppression of one group by another, typically involving routinised violence. The 'conflict' emerges clearly on the world stage only when the oppressed group finally takes up arms against the oppressor group, perhaps with wide moral support from the international community (subject to what form the violent resistance takes). In such situations (for example, in apartheid-era South Africa, or the ongoing displacement of Palestinians) the word 'conflict' may not be the best descriptor, implying as it might do that there is basically bilaterally equal responsibility for a situation which is based on the fact that something has been inflicted on one party. It will probably not be long, however, before the psychological damage caused to the 'inflicted upon' group will bring them to play their own part in cycles of retaliatory and gratuitous violence.

Like other forms of capital, emotional capital can be deployed or invested in different directions, depending on choices made at both individual and institutional levels. After a terrorist attack, or a disaster with fatalities, a lot of emotional effort may be invested in helping those traumatised or bereaved, e.g. through professional counsellors, community and volunteer initiatives, attentive media coverage, etc. This might help some of those affected, and society as a whole, to contain the emotional damage. But continuing terrorist attacks may stretch the emotional resources to a point where the sense of loss and of threat has become intolerable, and more defensive responses may ensue. Or over time, perhaps over generations, the emotional capital of a community may be depleted by persistent poverty and neglect, eroding the sense of both safety and dignity, and the capacity to contain. Many political problems can be seen as consequences of failures of containment, just as approaches to dealing with them need to call on the community's emotional capital.

'POPULISMS': A KIND OF EMOTIONAL INTELLIGENCE

It is not hard to see how the two principles of safety and dignity are currently playing an important role in the politics of many countries. Political commentary in recent years has become full of talk of 'populist' parties and leaders. In every continent there have been examples of surges in popular support for candidates whose ideologies and manifestos focus on restoring both safety and dignity to their national publics, and in some cases that support has been sufficient to carry those making these promises into government. Donald Trump's signature campaign promise to build a wall on the Mexican border offered a material symbolisation of safety, while the key slogan 'Make America Great Again' is clearly a demand for the restoration of a lost dignity. In Poland the name of the party currently in power echoes the two principles. The Law and Justice Party offers safety in laws defending traditional values (and in NATO), and claims dignity in the reclamation of Poland's Catholic heritage from the corruptions of communism. The surprising British majority vote (albeit by a very small margin) to leave the European Union appears to have been driven by fears that the free movement of labour was making Britain unsafe, and by a yearning for the dignity which some people felt they had lost as Britain became a post-industrial and less cohesive society.

This link in populist rhetorics between the principles of safety and dignity on the one hand, and culturally conservative and divisive politics on the other, may lead some people to be suspicious of a psychological approach which argues for the importance of those two principles. Surely we don't want politicians to be encouraging us to be fearful and preoccupied with safety. Nor do we want them pumping us up with unexamined pride. This is an important point, and sometimes a complex one, and we will encounter it again in his book. But the main point here is that politics has to address psychological realities as much as it does military and economic ones. Just a few decades ago, it would not have seemed likely that some 'inconvenient truths' about environmental change would be contesting for priority in political agendas. And in this psychological age, politics has to cope with a further major expansion of its core agendas. The global spread of democracy, the proliferation of media, and the rise of 'soft power', have added the inconvenience and intransigence of the human psyche to the list of political ineluctables.

Understanding what people feel, and why they feel it, is a core task of politics. If the experiences of safety and dignity are basic needs, then feelings of unsafety and of indignity will not melt away if they are ignored, not even if there are attempts to distract those suffering from them by pointing to other things which they should be glad of. In the British referendum of 2016, the Remain campaign, concentrating solely on economic arguments, completely failed to address those feelings. There was perhaps a failure to respond to the fact that many people could not see how EU membership brought them any economic benefit, but in any case this strategy could be described as emotionally illiterate: it failed to read the emotions of the public, which were such that for many people the economic arguments were not the most important.

In contrast, a key feature of populist politics is its tendency to home in precisely on feelings of unsafety and humiliation in sections of the public. Although in itself this falls far short of what we might properly call emotional intelligence, typically in its lack of empathy for other sections of the public, its dogmatisms and its sentimentalities, it could nonetheless be seen as having a degree of attunement to public feeling lacking in many other forms of contemporary political rhetoric.

THIS SHORT BOOK

In the chapters that follow we will consider how the two principles of safety and dignity, and the other core concepts of containment, defences, identity and narcissism, can be applied to three key topics: leaders, nations, and ideologies. The selection of these three areas reflects both their fundamental status in human society and also their particular prominence in contemporary politics. Still, it may seem like an old-fashioned list: what about social movements, climate change and the environment, the impact of social media on politics, etc.? These indeed are important topics, and there are others. Yet they all exist in a world in which we have leaders, we are citizens of nations, and we live in societies shaped by different ideas and values. Also, this is a short book, and much material that is fundamental and topical is not covered here. There are many sites at which we can work on understanding the connections between the great power and complexity of globalised political forces on the one hand, and the intricacies of the individual 'heart' and its development on the other. But hopefully those readers who find the broadly psychosocial, 'object-relations' approach presented here to be interesting will take away some ideas for thinking about the emotional heart of any area of politics.

2

LEADERS

RAGE AND RETRIBUTION

You bleed for those sons of a bitch. How many? Three thousand? I will kill more if only to get rid of drugs.[1]

When I say, 'I will kill you if you destroy my country', and 'I will kill you if you destroy the young of my country', I am asking everybody to find me a fault in those two statements.[2]

If I make it to the presidential palace I will do just what I did as mayor. You drug pushers, holdup men, and do-nothings, you better get out because I'll kill you.[3]

These are statements made during a successful campaign in 2016 by a candidate for election to the presidency of a country of more than 100 million people. Rodrigo Duterte is a middle-class, university-educated career politician, currently president of the Philippines, who was explaining his strategy for tackling the country's major drugs problem. He is an extreme example of a politician, well-known for the violence and misogyny of his language, but is head of state in one of the world's largest democracies. Later in this chapter we will discuss what responsibility leaders have for the climate of feeling in their countries – in this example, why is the rage about drug trafficking so focussed on savage retribution? But first we must walk through some more general ideas about, and analyses of, the dynamics of leadership.

AUTHORITY AND THE SUPEREGO

Leadership is a central issue in most aspects of human society, perhaps most obviously so in areas such as organisational life and politics. Yet it is one aspect of a wider and perhaps even deeper topic, that of authority. Authority is at the centre of all human relationships, including personal and intimate ones, because it is intrinsic to the questions of how we conduct ourselves, and how we make decisions; what rules we choose to follow, or to break; what standards we seek to achieve, or to subvert; what we expect of people, including ourselves. All such moral questions are at one level about authority, because they are about which or whose rules and standards we relate to, and about how we experience ourselves as moral agents able to act on our own authority.

These are not only questions about which people we respect and which codes we try to adhere to. They are also about a more subterranean area of human life, in which forms of pre-verbal relating to the world hold sway. These are laid down early in our psychological development, when we learn who or what to trust, and what we have to do to keep safe and to fit in with the world. In the technical language of psychoanalysis, it is the area of early superego development. The superego is that part of the mind in which the restraints and rules of the culture are embedded, transferred from one generation of superegos to the next (though with modifications along the way), and which is therefore core to our development as civilised beings. Out of the 'parental matrix', which was described in Chapter 1, there emerges a constellation of feelings and capacities in the developing person which we can call their 'superego', and which define that person's relationships with authority. This includes their own sense of personal authority, the capacity to make judgments and to act independently. So the superego is deeply linked to the individual's experience of both safety and dignity.

In the over-simplified versions of psychoanalysis sometimes found in general psychology textbooks, the term 'superego' can mean much the same as 'conscience'. It is usually painted in severe terms, as a punitive enforcer causing much painful guilt. Undoubtedly, guilt is a major source of pain, and the superego can in some persons be capable of great cruelty. However it is important to see it as a much broader and more complex region of the self, including not only fearful images of a forbidding censor, but also impressions of authority as caring and supportive. Indeed the capacity to feel guilt and remorse will not develop authentically if driven by fear alone, and needs a trusting and loving connection with whoever is doing the prohibiting or commanding.

What does all this early psychology have to do with the psychology of politics? The superego is a core part of the self which is not only an internal regulator but is also a set of powerful templates, deeply embedded in the adult mind and able to shape our experience throughout life of people and organisations we encounter which in one way or another represent authority to us. Our experiences of these authorities will carry the stamp of that early parental matrix, and any social institution or person carrying some meaning as a source of authority will occupy a quasi-parental place in the life of the adult citizen. Of course, that doesn't necessarily mean it will be trusted or followed. As we saw in Chapter 1, there is much ambivalence to be overcome in relationships with parents.

THE EXTERNALISED SUPEREGO

One of the earliest psychological theories of leadership is still a rich source of understanding its dynamics. It was set out by Sigmund Freud in his 1921 essay on group psychology. He noted that when individuals inhabit a collective identity, they merge a part of themselves into that identity. The part in question is what Freud a little later came to call the 'superego'. His crucial observation was that group members were often prepared to hand over their superego functions, at least in part, to the leader of the group, and so were prepared to act in ways that as individuals they would probably not allow themselves. Group membership is therefore a reversal of the process of emotional maturation. Having spent the years of growing up in efforts to internalise restraint, and to build our own internal capacity for self-regulation, we project that back out there, to someone (or something) in the external world, when we commit to a group which is emotionally significant to us. In return for this loss of full selfhood, of psychic autonomy, the individual can gain the safety and the dignity of belonging to a group, under the protection and blessing of its leader. This experience may however be illusory, and so be a long-term threat to the well-being of the individual. Moreover, there is another more obviously dangerous consequence of this dynamic of group membership, in that group members may find themselves acting on feelings or impulses which are destructive or self-damaging.

There are many ways in which this dynamic can play out, with very different consequences, depending on what feelings the group leader is giving permission to group members to release, or what actions the leader is demanding of the group. In criminal gang cultures, the permission or demand may often be for violent behaviour. In bohemian communes, it may be for promiscuity and other hedonistic activities. In political parties or movements, it is a demand for belief in what the organisation stands for, and for action to promote its aims. The content of that demand will vary according to the ideology involved. The demands may conceal permissions as well – to engage in antagonistic behaviour, for example, perhaps even violence, or to take yourself away from your relationships with family or friends.

As was noted in Chapter 1, we are more familiar with the negative versions of this phenomenon. Freud's model of group dynamics has influenced many attempts to explain the rise of Nazism and the Holocaust. Indeed, a general implication of the model is that group membership is intrinsically a form of diminished selfhood, a condition into which people with less integrated superegos (i.e. less psychic maturity) are more likely to fall. Freud was influenced by the rise of totalitarianism, in response to which he and many other intellectuals held a suspicion of the collective and an idealisation of the autonomous, fully self-possessed individual who would be less vulnerable to the seductions of leaders.

However, developments in psychoanalytic thinking since Freud about the superego and about groups enable us to expand his model such that we can see leader-follower or leader-public relationships in terms of a wide range of possibilities. Our perceptions of and feelings about leaders may be the result of various aspects of the self being projected onto them, with different elements in leaders' personalities acting as the hook or target for those projections. So to an important degree, we create our leaders through projection. But a leader must be willing and able to inhabit and to own the projected feelings and identities.

What about the leaders themselves? The choice to become a political leader may, in the person's internal unconscious, be an attempt to inhabit a superego role in the external world. At its worst, this might mean gaining the power to inflict on others whatever punishments the person feels they have been threatened with by their own superego. (Our discussion of terrorism in Chapter 4 will explore that scenario.) At its best, it might mean the leader becoming a benign and protective authority, thereby either reproducing their own good developmental experiences of superego figures, or filling a gap in their personal development. Justin Frank's (2012) psychoanalytic study of Barack Obama links both merits and flaws in his leadership style to – amongst other factors – his early loss of a father. His parents separated when he was one, and his father moved away. In later life, including in his role as president, Obama sought to be the father he had missed while also being very ambivalent in his relationship with his internal image of father.

There are a number of 'psychobiographies' of leaders which try to trace their emotional development and its shaping of their adult characters, and to examine the fit (or sometimes the lack of fit) between the person and the office occupied, with its political demands and opportunities to respond to the emotional profile of the public. Some recent American presidents have been the subject of interesting psychobiographies; as well as Frank's study of Obama, and an earlier one by him of George W. Bush, there is also one by Vamik Volkan on Richard Nixon's very difficult childhood and his subsequent narcissism and self-destructiveness (Volkan et al., 1997).

In the rest of this chapter we will however focus more on the 'followership' side of leadership. We will consider how broad changes in society have affected leadership styles, by modifying what we want and need to see in leaders. These changes bring the psychological dimensions of leader-follower relations more into focus. We will discuss the question of whether leaders are made in the image of their followers, or vice versa. Then we will look at some examples of how leaders respond to their public's needs for safety and dignity, and of what containment they can offer of the anxieties around those needs.

AMBIVALENCE TOWARDS AUTHORITY

Perhaps the most obvious form of authority in everyday life is that of the law. The law is easily pictured both as an external superego in both a patriarchal, punitive mode, as something designed to oppress rather than protect us, and also as a fundamentally benign source of collective strength and rectitude. There may be many specific situations in external reality which fit one or the other of these dichotomised images of a 'good' law and a 'bad' one. We may consume, in rapid succession, media reports about the heroism of some police officers and the corruption of others. An 'official' and widely shared rhetoric about the goodness of the law and those employed to enforce it exists alongside many narratives that assume the opposite. This cultural ambivalence towards the law reflects the mixed nature of reality, but also echoes the ambivalence towards parental authority which is especially noticeable in adolescence and its oscillations between needy dependence and resentful hostility.

The psychological basis of ambivalence towards authority, in the process of development from infancy through adolescence, is present in us all, though as individuals we are able to resolve it to varying degrees, and express either or both sides of it in endlessly varying ways. These will be strongly influenced by our social environments. It seems that social media have hugely expanded the scope for public expression of negative feelings about politicians, sometimes testing the legal proscription of hate speech. However there is reason to think that expression of the negative side of the ambivalence was gaining strength some decades before social media, due to a number of factors but in particular the broad cultural trend over at least the last half century of falling levels of trust in traditional institutions and professions, and growing scepticism about some types of expertise. Politicians have been especially affected by the weakening of deferential trust in their integrity and competence. They are the least trusted profession in the UK, according to IpsosMORI's annual Veracity Index of 2017,[4] which reports that only 17% of the public trust them to tell the truth.

Globally, the overall picture of trust in politics is complex. Trust in politicians is not quite the same as trust in government, and both differ from trust in political institutions, so recorded levels of trust in politics will depend on the questions asked. And as the 2018 Edelman Trust Barometer shows,[5] there are international year-by-year variations, with some countries such as Argentina, France and Germany showing surprising increases in trust in government since 2012, with fluctuations in between. So some positive attitudes towards authorities remain, but negative ones towards politicians are probably on a long-term rising trend, with some people becoming relentlessly disparaging of them. To be cynical about politics ('I don't trust any of them') seems to have become for many people a criterion of basic worldliness. Amongst other people, positive attitudes may be inflated to the point of idealisation, in denial of a disappointing reality. If we try to understand all this psychologically, we can see it as regressive splitting, a difficulty in holding on to a complex, mixed view of vital social institutions, instead retreating to the simplicities of a black-and-white world. This may suggest that some erosion of our general capacity to trust has occurred, a diminution of emotional capital in society as a whole. In representative democracies, there is obviously risk to the democratic process when attitudes towards elected politicians are dominated by splitting and the negative side of the ambivalence is becoming stronger, a situation facilitating the rise of 'populist' leaders.

THE CHANGING STYLES OF LEADERSHIP: INFORMAL, EMOTIONAL, PERSONAL

Another cultural trend of relevance to understanding the changing dynamics of leader-follower relations has been called the informalisation of everyday life (the sociologist Cas Wouters [2007] has led the way in defining this trend). This refers to the fact that social formalities and conventions, including those related to differences in status and authority, no longer regulate social exchanges to the extent that they used to. For example, dress codes are much more relaxed than they were, and less indicative of rank. First name address is common even across wide gaps in age and status. This trend may sometimes mislead by obscuring the hierarchies that continue to exist, but overall must surely be a positive development: it signals that respect should flow 'down' as well as 'up', it may reduce the timidity of younger or more junior people, and it facilitates inclusiveness. It can reduce the distance between politicians and the people, though politicians must be careful in this area, since as they know, affecting an informality which does not come naturally can make for bad publicity.

Informalisation is linked to two other broad cultural changes which are impacting on political leadership: personalisation and emotionalisation. Emotionalisation is a complex cultural phenomenon which is linked to the rise of psychology we noted earlier. At its core is an increase in emotional expressivity in everyday life, but amongst many other things it also involves an increased popular interest in emotional experience, and in the intimate lives of celebrities and public figures. Leaders are now permitted a much wider range of emotional expression than previously – in fact, this is now desired of them. The changing leadership styles in a more emotionalised culture have been explored in Candida Yates' study of British political culture from the late 1990s to 2015. The public's interest is partly served by, and partly generates, media content in which politicians are presented as emotional persons as well as, or even rather than, the bearers of policies.

The trend to personalisation is therefore closely linked to emotionalisation. There has been a tendency amongst politicians and commentators in the more stable democracies to underplay the importance of leaders. What matters, we have often been told, is policies not personalities. It is as if an attraction to individual leaders sets us on a dangerous path which could lead again to the horrors of twentieth-century fascism. Yet this fear sits in a cultural environment in which there are endless invitations in our media to experience and consider politicians as persons, and to focus on the personalities of our leaders. Two developments have facilitated this personalisation of politics.

One is the process of 'dealignment' – the dissolution of the links between socio-economic position and political affiliation. While in the past the industrial working class could have been expected to vote *en masse* for parties of the left, the dissolution of clear and stable class structures has led to much more complex and unpredictable patters of voting. Ideologies grounded in class identity have much weaker influence, and the 'Left-Right' distinction can no longer organise the diversity of political opinion. In this context, more space is available for the personal qualities of candidates to become important in electoral choice.

The second is to be found in socio-technical developments in media. The arrival of television in the 1950s and 1960s brought the personal presence of politicians into everyday experience. The first televised debate between presidential candidates in the US, between John Kennedy and Richard Nixon in 1960, was seen as a turning point in the campaign. Kennedy subsequently won the election by a narrow margin, with many commentators and polls suggesting this was due at least in part to his much more telegenic presence and performance in the debate. The later rise of the web and of social media, and of the global 24-hour news environment, have afforded deeper audience involvement in many aspects of politics, with the domain of emotional responses to politicians expanding and being of focal interest for many people. There some negative sides to this. The intensive visual presentation of leaders on television and online can have distracting or trivialising effects on political debate, and it may negatively affect the leadership prospects of very capable people who do not have distinctive screen appeal.

However, while this is clearly a mixed development, we might welcome it as being more positive than sinister. It can help to sustain public interest in politics, in times when the sterile ritualism of party competition and the remoteness of political elites has turned large numbers of people away from it. What interests many people most is other people, and what matters most are our relationships with other people. Passionately focussed though some people are on issues like the environment or human rights, productive emotional engagement with politics is for many most likely to develop when it is somehow personalised. This may come about through an issue being dramatised by the case of an individual (say, stories of an individual migrant, CEO or terrorist coming to represent the broad issues of migration, business governance or terror), or through the media presence of an appealing leader (or perhaps through an aversive response to an unappealing one).

Many members of the public have perhaps always ignored the advice to stick to policies, and have instead been heavily influenced by how they relate to leaders and aspiring leaders as people, even though they mostly have only 'para-social' contact with them (i.e. via the media) so that relating is based on impressions gained from media content alone. Certainly, before the age of television some leaders were acutely aware of their emotional impact on their followers, and of how their personal character and its presentation was crucial to their political support. Reflecting this, in the classic sociological theory of charisma, academics have also registered the power of the emotional tie between leader and follower. For the sociologist Max Weber in 1919,[6] the appeal of the charismatic leader rested on personal qualities, distinguishing that style of leadership from 'traditional' and 'bureaucratic' types, which were based on respect for roles defined by custom and by law respectively (say, tribal elder or high court judge) not on the emotional appeal of a person. Perhaps academic theory, which across the social sciences this century has been undergoing a 'turn to affect', is only now just returning to Weber and catching up with reality. Yet reality is also moving, and political leadership is becoming more explicitly personalised and emotionalised, as is culture as a whole.

THE LEADERS WE DESERVE?

This focus on the emotional dynamics of leadership points to a way of answering the old and fundamental question of whether – for better or worse – we get the leaders we deserve. In societies with some degree of functioning democracy it is hard to avoid the conclusion that yes, we do – though in a limited sense, as we will see. While the capacity of wealthy and influential elites to manipulate elections through propaganda and other forms of influence, if not outright corruption, should not be underestimated, voters usually have some choice, and exercise it. On this view, leaders may articulate public opinion, but do not radically shape it.

Insofar as we do exercise choice, it is not in the simple way that rationalist models of democracy would have it. Rational and evidence-based comparative analysis of policy alternatives on offer may play a part amongst some voters, but 'voter competence' levels (how much electorates know about the issues and can make rational, informed judgments about them) are not high even in the most educated societies. So recourse to an intuitive summary judgment of candidates is common, and is likely to be heavily influenced by a voter's emotional responses to the candidates. As we've observed, their judgments may be based on what voters project of themselves onto the public personae of candidates, and therefore on how much they can identify or feel a bond with one candidate more than others, or on how much they are repulsed by a candidate onto whom they have projected some very negative qualities. Or voters may be searching out the candidate who they feel can best meet their needs to feel, say, more safe or more respected. In these circumstances, the successful candidate may likely be the one who, irrespective of competence and even of ideology, has a public persona which best fits the emotional needs of a crucial segment of the public.[7] So we the public are choosing, albeit for what may be largely unconscious reasons, the candidate whom we have ourselves largely constructed. Some would see the role of the media as crucial in that process of construction, although again there is a debate to be had about whether we get the media we deserve. Do the media simply articulate public emotion, or shape it?

LEADING BY EXAMPLE

Let's continue to test the view that neither the media nor leaders actually create their publics, but simply reflect them. Is this true at moments of crisis, when there may be clear choices available to leaders about how to lead? There are always different structures of feeling[8] present in the pool of public emotion, and at times of acute disturbance and uncertainty when leaders are looked to for guidance they may be able to choose which of these to express and support. After a major terrorist attack, for example, there is grief, fear, rage and resolve, and leaders' choice of language in the aftermath shapes and modulates some of these feelings more than others, with differing consequences on a number of fronts, especially in relation to social cohesion and to support for counter-terrorism policies. Two days after 77 terrorist murders in Oslo and on the island of Utoya in Norway in July 2011, the then Norwegian Prime Minister Jens Stoltenberg in a national memorial address spoke powerfully about the victims, and then struck a remarkably positive note of optimistic resolve.

> Amidst all this tragedy, I am proud to live in a country that has managed to hold its head up high at a critical time. I have been impressed by the dignity, compassion and resolve I have met. We are a small country, but a proud people. We are still shocked by what has happened, but we will never give up our values. Our response is more democracy, more openness, and more humanity. But never naïvety. No one has said it better than the Labour Youth League girl who was interviewed by CNN: 'If one man can create that much hate, you can only imagine how much love we as a togetherness can create'.[9]

We can compare this with the quotations at the start of this chapter, a few of the many statements made by the Rodrigo Duterte about the ongoing crisis of massive drug use in his country, the Philippines. The contrast between these two leaders demonstrates the fundamental role of public emotion in shaping leadership. Neither set of statements could conceivably have been made by a national leader in the other country. So something about Norwegian culture and its shaping of the psychology of the Norwegian public produced the Stoltenberg statement, while making it impossible for the Duterte statements to have been uttered in Norway. Nor could Duterte's violence have been released amongst the Philippino public without their substantial collusion. In fact, with his reputation and style as a political leader already established from years as a mayor, he received 16.6 million votes, 39% of the votes cast, in his victory in the presidential election of 2016.

However these examples also indicate the role of individual leaders in giving voice to reserves of particular feeling at particular times. There are politicians in Norway who after Utoya would have spoken in a different tone from that adopted by Stoltenberg. While subscribing to the general horror at this atrocity, the anti-immigration Norwegian Progress Party had a different version of the resolution not to be led into losing its values: it affirmed the importance of retaining its policy priorities. And of course there are many in the Philippines who speak differently from Duterte on how to deal with the drug problem, including Benigno Aquino III, who lost the presidency to Duterte.

Stoltenberg's speech had a strong effect on the Norwegian public, who rallied around his words, and his approval ratings improved considerably. This was not a long-term effect, but the speech seemed to play a major role in containing public feeling during a critical period. However, the difficulty for national leaders is that national publics are emotionally diverse, and finding an appropriate response for all the feelings that may be present in the public at the time is an impossible task. Still, good emotional governance requires as wide a containing response as possible. The speech did not address the fear and the rage which many Norwegians must have been feeling, even if they did so against their better judgment. The Oslo/Utoya attack was a major assault on the sense of safety, and on the dignity of Norway as peaceable and cohesive country. The prime minister's speech tended to idealise the Norwegian public as extraordinarily resolute, leaving little space for anything more complicated or ambivalent to be expressed. It followed a claim that this was not naïve with a statement that could be seen as naïve. All this may explain why its unifying effect was short-lived. Most people urgently wanted to regain the experience of safety and dignity, and Stoltenberg's words offered a noble way towards that. As such they offered some containment of the shock and anxiety, in modelling a composed and resilient response. To speak at all at such a time must be extremely hard, and this was a deeply felt and eloquent speech. It would be unrealistic to expect one speech to give voice to all reactions to the killings. In the longer run, however, a more variegated picture of the Norwegian public would need to be presented if the polarising forces which had given rise to the attacks were to be more comprehensively managed and contained.

Duterte also must have 'struck a chord', though in the opposite of a containing way. How can a national presidential candidate brag of murdering people, and then be elected? The Philippines does not only have a drug problem; it also has a major terrorism problem. In the year before Duterte's election as president, several groups with allegiance to or similar aims as ISIS were involved in bombings, burning of villages, extortion, kidnappings and beheadings. The police have been unable to deal with the problem, so the army was continuously deployed against the terrorist paramilitaries, who were especially strong in the region Duterte came from. Later, in 2017, Islamist fighters actually took control of a city in the south of the country, and a military battle involving nearly a thousand deaths was necessary to reclaim it. The country's politics for most of its history have been turbulent and bloody, and the thousands of extra-judicial killings in Duterte's war on drugs are integral to its violent history. This is the kind of situation where one would expect emotional capital to be at very low levels, with the sense of safety seriously depleted, and dignity minimal except in privileged strata of the population. In that context, it is plausible that a population habituated to violence, yet also desperate to escape it, might turn to a violent leader promising to demolish one key part of the ruin that is their society. Potentials for (often sexualised) violence therefore awaited the arrival of a Duterte, though his particular character was perhaps also necessary to break the taboo on a president openly glorifying and promising violence.

At the moments of potential flux occasioned by an election, it is very possible for an incumbent to be replaced by a very different leader, perhaps quite suddenly. This reminds us that a public is never monolithic – there are bodies of feeling present in it other than that expressed in the current regime, such that given the availability of a potential leader with a different emotional appeal and an effective way of communicating it, one of these other structures of feeling may take hold of government. So while leaders must work within the psychological limits of their publics, they can play crucial roles in the complex processes which bring about switches of government from one emotional base to another, by mobilising a particular constituency of feeling, a particular segment of the emotional public. As was suggested in the previous chapter, the 'leave' campaigners in the UK's 2016 'Brexit' referendum were able to do this, by an articulation of anxieties about the loss of British identity or its dignity, and thus overturning a long-standing (if narrow) majority of public sentiment in favour of remaining in Europe.

So we should not overlook the active role of the leader in making history. Leaders are not only chosen by the public to act out the collective will, and it would be misleading for us to rest with a simple assertion that therefore we get the leaders we deserve. A national public is a hugely complex phenomenon, psychologically, so much so that to speak of a 'national psyche' is bound to be a major simplification. Many different structures of feeling within it are available for mobilisation, and through their words, images and deeds some political leaders will, deliberately or not, be working to identify and bring some of those structures to the surface and to foreground or amplify some feelings rather than others. So we have come to the overall conclusion that publics and leaders make each other; there are endless complex interactions involving expressed feelings and unconscious phantasies amongst the public, their representations in mainstream and social media, the internal worlds (the motives and perceptions) of political leaders at all levels, and the external world demands of economic life, diplomacy, and so on. While the default position in psychoanalysis is more towards seeing people as responsible for managing their own feelings, perhaps in the political context we should give a little more emphasis to the opportunities that leaders have to influence how their publics do this, and to help build up emotional capital.

LEADING INTO BATTLE

This influence of leadership may be most clear, and most consequential, in some conflict situations, especially those of potential violence, military or other. Alongside the classical non-psychological causes of inter- and intranational conflicts (such as who governs a territory and its people, or has access to its resources), there are the psychosocial processes by which our internal needs and anxieties fasten themselves onto some aspects of the conflict and rigidify the minds of those involved. The Israeli psychologist Daniel Bar-Tal (2013) has developed the concept of 'conflictive ethos' to describe a situation in which, whatever is objectively at stake in the conflict, the parties involved have come to experience it in certain ways. For example, they see it as *fundamental* to their identity, and as a zero-sum affair, such that any benefit to their enemy must be a loss to themselves. Those and other related perceptions lock them into pursuit of the conflict, and paradoxically enable them to bear it carrying on, so that it then becomes intractable. In a different theoretical language, Vamik Volkan, through many studies of conflicts around the world, and the roles of leaders within them, has written about how a process of 'large group regression' can take place, involving the majority of people in a society and resulting in the intractability which Bar-Tal describes.

This is most likely to happen when a leader emerges whose own personality is dominated by a malignant narcissism, and who encourages large sections of the public into regressed states of mind in which the world is grossly simplified. The large group's identity (typically that of a 'nation') is idealised, and the process of splitting, on which that idealisation depends, also produces demonised enemies, and a number of other adverse effects. A large group is vulnerable to this process, says Volkan, when it is unable to process and tolerate the level of anxiety to which its members are subject. In terms of the ideas which are outlined in this book, this would mean that an insufficient experience of safety and/or dignity has raised levels of anxiety to a point at which the group will seek a defensive response. This is offered by a leader who promises safety and dignity, linked in more toxic cases to an image of a purified national community, of which more below.

THE 'POPULIST' PHENOMENON

Much discussion of political leadership around the world in recent years has focussed on the concept of 'populism'. Typically this involves a charismatic leader who seeks power on the basis of offering an end to politics as we know it. This leader is presented as of a new type, either because s/he is not a professional politician, or is one who somehow claims exclusively to know and understand the 'people' and promises to champion them against the political 'establishment', the 'elite' who have been in power for so long and achieved so little. There is an overlap with the much older category of 'strong man' leader, the protecting father who is not a populist in today's sense but in whom the 'people' have a confidence that transcends their broken trust in political institutions and democratic process.

Not all forms of contemporary populism are of the 'Right': 'Left' populisms can and do occur, as the era of Chavez and Maduro in Venezuela can be seen to illustrate, and perhaps also the 2016 electoral campaigns of Corbyn and Sanders in the UK and US respectively, though neither of these posed a sharp 'us the people vs. the elite' dichotomy. Syriza in Greece and Podemos in Spain are seen by some as examples of 'Left' populism, while the Five Star Movement (M5S) in Italy defies placing on that axis (which as we have noted is of limited usefulness in describing politics today). Leftist populism can be seen as at least partially adhering to the principles of safety and dignity, though in different ways to Rightist versions: material security rather than border security is often the guarantee of safety, via state provision for health and welfare, while dignity may also be materially defined in terms of better pay, secure employment and housing, rather than being seen culturally.

One feature which all varieties of 'populism', including the M5S, have in common, and which therefore is often taken in academic discussions of the term to be its defining characteristic, is a deep disaffection with the political 'establishment'. The populist leader's appeal is that of the outsider, someone untainted by the complacency or corruption of the elite, someone who can be in touch with the 'people', and so really offers something different. Psychologically, this is the wish for purity, a narcissistic impulse of reaching for the perfect world, in response to a collapse of trust in politics in the real world. As such, the enthusiasm for the new order, the 'Golden Dawn' promised by the extremist party of that name in Greece, is condemned to eventual collapse, as the promise of purity cannot be delivered.

The extent to which contemporary populism is a new development in leader-follower relations is debatable. Has there not for a long time been an us vs. them at the heart of human society, ready to be stirred up by leaders who believe in themselves as forces of renewal, and now more easily stirred via the direct and fevered channels of social media? Or are we seeing a new kind of leadership, facilitated by modern communications but with a new emotional dynamic?

At the psychological level, there is nothing new about today's populisms. Their basic dynamic appears to be one in which the parental figures (the incumbent political class, the 'elite') are felt to have comprehensively failed, even to have betrayed those for whom they are responsible. A deep, amorphous anger fills the political air and people feel various combinations of abandoned, deceived and exploited. As we saw in Chapter 1, feelings of distrust and rage against parental figures of early life are universal. So how can we understand the rise of cynicism and anger in popular attitudes towards politics, to the point where elections are won by parties or leaders whose key promise is to overthrow the establishment, to replace the actual, bad parents with an ideal, good one?

For many, economic recession is the key explanation, bringing as it does attacks on the well-being and dignity of the unemployed and the low waged, and a sense of insecurity to many others. Others see globalisation and rapid cultural change as the main problem, disrupting the stable communities which offered a sense of safety and self-respect. So combine austerity regimes with the surge in migration, and you may have the two crises which bring to a head long-standing popular disaffection at the underlying trends of growing inequality and increasing globalisation. There may seem to be little need for expert psychology to contribute to understanding where the swell of anger comes from.

But there is still important psychological work to do. Nations similarly affected by the two crises have responded in different ways, which psychosocial analysis may help to explain. And the specific content and focus of public feeling in individual countries is important to understand. Just how do people experience their difficulties, what troubles them most, who do they blame, what do they want most? The core argument of this book would suggest that the central issues are ones of safety and dignity: somehow people feel that their societies now are unsafe for them, and do not endow them with dignity. Without reliable understanding of the emotional profiles of regressive populist movements, it is difficult for political leaders opposing them to develop the best strategies for doing so.

Also, feelings of safety and dignity are gained and lost in many areas of life, not only in the political sphere. What changes might there have been at deeper levels of society, in family life and everyday culture, and in the various societal provisions that bear on early development, which may have been impacting on our early experience and making us more insecure in our core emotional selves? At least since the 1970s, there have been suggestions that, for various reasons, the presence in many societies of narcissistic traits has been increasing. If that is so, then even without economic crisis and cultural fragmentation there would be an increasing need amongst the public for leaders who would collude with or invite narcissistic defences, and promise painlessly and simply to deliver the safety and dignity which people feel they lack.

AND SO TO TRUMP AND KIM JONG-UN

Speaking of which, at the time of writing the most obvious and consequential example of a populist leader is Donald Trump, elected as
president of the US in 2016. Trump, perhaps like Duterte, also elected
in 2016, and some others in the wave of populist arrivals, brings a
new dimension to the idea of personalised politics. The idea of 'personalisation' as we encountered it earlier usually refers to the way
in which citizens 'consume' their politics, with the personalities or
personas of leaders being of as much or more interest to voters than
the policies they are attached to and the parties and ideologies they
represent. It is something that happens in the media sphere, and it
reflects an important change in how citizens relate to their political
leaders, as well as in the increased attention which many politicians
pay to their appearance and social behaviour. But Trump seems to have
brought his personality through and beyond style into the content of
politics, so that strategy and sometimes objectives are defined by who
he is. So there is a mutation of leadership best described not as personalisation but as a 'personisation' of statecraft, similar in some ways
to a kind of autocracy. To some extent, in Trump's case this involves a
fragmentation of strategy and objectives, due to his emotional lability
and superficiality and also, a recent report by Bob Woodward suggests,[10] to ad hoc restraints which some of those around him are able
to impose.

Thus when Donald Trump met Kim Jong-Un in June 2018, it was
not a summit in the usual sense of the term, that is, a meeting at
which the participants represent large and complex bodies of strategic interests and expertise. This was a meeting that somehow sprang
from the self-centred calculations of two highly narcissistic individuals, aided it seems by more conventional diplomatic efforts on the
part of South Korea to transform the unhappy situation on the Korean
Peninsula. The calculations of the two men converged in that both saw
a dramatic mould-breaking meeting being to their individual advan-
tage. It would not actually have to change anything, but would enable
each to offer their own people a better world, any subsequent failure

of which to arrive could later be blamed on the other, or explained in some other way (perhaps riskier for Trump as the US has free media).

The meeting in Singapore was an encounter between the two major types of narcissism of the twentieth century, continuing into the present. Trump embodies the narcissistic tendency inherent in market-based societies, while Kim is the apotheosis of the collectivised form of narcissism generated by totalitarian societies. But the psychological root of each man is the same. We must remind ourselves that narcissism is not a simple excess of self-regard, but a defence against fear, against what would otherwise be an overwhelming internal sense of vulnerability and weakness. It is a mode of experience in which the intrinsic dependency of the self on others is so terrifying that it has to be denied. We all engage in this manoeuvre to some extent, but when narcissism becomes the founding principle of a personality, the fear against which it defends is firmly sealed off in the unconscious.

Trump's contemptuous intolerance of the complexities and uncertainties of politics was clear in the abrupt and aggressive manner of his departure from the G7 summit en route to the Singapore meeting, which was more of his own, simpler design, based on the performance of success rather than its achievement. Narcissism in leaders does not necessarily bring disaster; on the contrary, some measure of it may be necessary for the self-belief required to succeed in the arduous work of progressive politics. But for that to happen the leader's narcissistic self must be identified with some ideal of the common good — a vision of real reconciliation, say, in a leader whose task is to resolve a conflict. In the cases of Trump and Kim, their narcissistic selves appear to be expressed through visions of their own importance as paragons of what they believe their societies to be about — Trump, the feral property developer; Kim, the dynastic godhead. In this case, whatever the consequences of the 'summit', it demonstrated that in this psychological age, the importance of a psychological understanding of politics has never been so great.

3

NATIONS

NATIONS AND NATIONALISMS

Human civilisation is presently organised into nations, 193 of them on the current count of United Nations member states. Some commentators think the end of the nation is in sight: national governments are overwhelmed from without by the global forces of finance capital, multinational corporations and consumer culture, and undermined from within by increasingly divided and disaffected populations, less willing to tolerate self-serving or corrupt ruling elites. Viewed politically and economically, many nations do seem to be in shaky condition. But what about the psychology of nations? Are our attachments to them waning as a direct reflection of globalisation? And as we see in many nations the rise of aggressive and regressive nationalisms, do we think that the sooner nationalism is part of history, the better?

Here we will examine some key themes in the psychology of nationalism. We will unavoidably confront the worst of nationalism, which can be a very toxic force, and sometimes a psychotic one. However, we will also find some more positive qualities and potentials in it, and end with the suggestion that viewed psychologically, the problem now is not basically that there is an excess of nationalism, but that there is not enough nationalism of the right sort.

Firstly, some definitions. By nationalism, we will mean a state of mind in which there is:

a   A sense of belonging to a particular nation (national identity);
b   An emotional attachment to that identity;
c   A political concern for the interests of the nation and its people.

This definition begs all sorts of questions, particularly about how a nationalist will relate to the peoples of other nations. It does not assume that nationalists will always see politics *primarily* in terms of national interests, nor that they will always want to prioritise the interests of their *own* nation. This definition would probably find 'nationalist' feeling in many people who would not want to be called 'nationalists', some of whom might prefer that we called them 'patriots'. These semantics are very important, though we cannot go into them further here. The rationale for this broad definition is that the nature and strength of nationalism as a political force will depend on the full spectrum of feelings about the nation amongst its population, and many of these feelings are very different from those associated with xenophobic and aggressive forms of nationalism.

There is one other definition we must consider. What do we mean by a 'nation', the object of nationalist feeling? There is a large and complex body of scholarship in the social sciences on this question, which we will dip into here in a very restricted and simplifying way. Early theories emerging in the nineteenth century saw nations as the natural products of long histories, reaching powerfully and deeply into the minds of their peoples. These theories may be called '*essentialist*', because they see the nation as having an essence, a definitive core, from which its meaning for us derives. On this view, nationalist feeling flows naturally from the inherent meaningfulness and venerability of the nation. In the most emphatic view of this sort, nations are part of the fundamental natural order of things, a view described as 'primordialist' by one of the leading theorists of the nation and nationalism, Anthony Smith.

Essentialist theories of the nation and its ancient roots were rejected later in the twentieth century by a second wave of theories, called 'modernist' by Smith (2009) because they see nations as the product of the 'modern' period of history, to have come into being from the seventeenth or eighteenth century on, without older historical roots. Various accounts have been given of this process, for example, those emphasising the role of capitalist economic development and competition, or those which focus on the role of nationalisms as reactions to global imperialism. In recent decades perhaps the most influential have been what we can call 'constructionist' accounts, according to which nations have emerged as a consequence of particular socio-cultural changes. Foremost amongst these are the theories of political scientist Benedict Anderson (1983) and philosopher/anthropologist Ernest Gellner (1983), who considered the emerging forces of, respectively, print media in the eighteenth century and public education systems in the nineteenth century as major origins of national consciousness in the first modern nations. While a people may have lived under the same jurisdiction, they did not know they were a 'nation' until their schools or their newspapers told them who they were. In analyses of this sort, a sense of national identity and unity is to some extent an artefact. It is an imaginary construction which has been engineered in people's minds, whether as a by-product of other developments or as part of a deliberate strategy intended somehow to serve the interests of political or economic elites.[1]

Illuminating and important though modernist theories may be, from a psychological point of view we have to agree with Smith's judgment that they are limited by their neglect of the powerful affective dimensions of nations and nationalism, a power seen abundantly in international contests in sport, in diverse forms of political rhetoric, and in many wars. There is a crucial *imaginative* component in all our social experiences – a principle at the heart of the approach taken in this book – but it is hard to explain the depth and intensity of national feeling if we see the nation as an artifice, which can be de-constructed and de-mystified. While there are many determinedly cosmopolitan people who opt out of national identities, viewed globally it seems that essentialist views capture more of the psychological reality of popular experiences of the nation.

THE ETHNIC-CIVIC DISTINCTION IN THEORIES OF NATIONALISM

In the social-scientific literature on nationalism there has been much discussion of what some have seen as a distinction between its ethnic and civic forms. The former can be loosely linked to essentialist theories of the nation, in that it is the kind of nationalism you would expect to find amongst citizens who held a broadly essentialist view of their nation. The ethnic type of nationalism typically reveres the nation as a strongly defined community stretching back through the generations, with a specific way of life and shared values. People use the term differently, but 'ethnic' can mean pertaining to culture, rather than its current meaning in everyday and administrative languages of 'racial' group, as in the terms 'ethnicity' and 'ethnic minority'. So we might see an 'ethnic' nationalism as defining its nation's essence by culture and territory rather than blood and lineage. The US is a very strong example of this. But ethnic nationalisms frequently tend to restrictive, racialised definitions, and can be co-opted into divisive and xenophobic political stances. They have often given nationalism a bad name amongst liberal and cosmopolitan publics.

The civic type of nationalism can be linked, though only partially, to modernist theories. In the purest civic models of nationalism, there is no organic body of culture or tradition which the citizen must feel part of. Positive feeling about the nation is in the form of respect for its present laws and institutions, and is expressed in the form of participation, however minimal, in its democratic processes. It is a cool, Enlightenment style of nationalism, with an appealing inclusivity. Anyone can choose to adopt the identity of a nation by living in it and abiding by its laws. Attachment to the nation is basically rational and pragmatic, contractual rather than visceral. A believer in a modernist theory of nations might see this as the most appropriate way of relating to one's nation (although another modernist response would be to turn away altogether from what may be seen as the whole fraudulent business of nationhood and nationalism).

THE NATION AS A MODERN PASSION

The psychology of a purely civic nationalism would be much less dramatic than that of ethnic varieties. Indeed, it may require very little psychological explanation beyond a model of rational behaviour. However, many writers have argued that there is no such as thing as a purely 'civic' nation, that there is always some form of cultural community inside lived experiences of the nation, and that the ethnic-civic dichotomy is therefore a false one, since ethnicity at least in a cultural sense is always present.

However, this does not mean that modernist theories of the nation are wrong. There are many reasons to see our modern nations as modern phenomena, and a psychosocial approach requires us to understand things in their socio-historical context. So we need to combine some sort of 'modernist' approach to understanding how and when nations developed with an appreciation of the power of what may seem to be ancient, and sometimes regressive, qualities in the emotional attachments many people have to them.

We have a starting point for this task in a third type of answer to the question 'What is a nation?', the type which seeks to combine the useful elements of essentialist and modernist theories. Smith, for example, set out an alternative paradigm which he called ethno-symbolism. He suggested that modern nations have typically formed around pre-existing communities which he called 'ethnies'. Although strongly shaped by genealogical descent, these communities were basically cultural ones, defined by myths of common ancestry, shared historical memories, and elements of everyday culture (such as language or religion) symbolically linked to a particular homeland territory. When modern nations were formed, the major ethnies they incorporated were the sources of their majority cultures.

This historical perspective recognises national identity both as an authentic dimension of self-experience, and as a major territory of public feeling which will be the subject of intense political competition and manipulation. Smith, and some other writers, have thus occupied the theoretical space between essentialism and modernism, showing the inadequacy of those polar positions and setting a background for in-depth psychological investigation.

THE DISTRIBUTION OF DIGNITY FOR ALL

As a bridge into fully psychological territory, we must refer to the work of another leading theorist of the nation and nationalism. Liah Greenfeld[2] offers a very different historical account from that of Smith, on the face of it a very modernist one (albeit *early* modernist). She argues that the idea of the nation was born in the aftermath of the Wars of the Roses in fifteenth-century England. Those protracted and bloody wars, between two royal 'houses' contending for the throne of England, had decimated the ruling aristocracy. So when Henry VII emerged as the victorious king and established the Tudor dynasty, it was necessary to repopulate the ruling elite (on whom the monarch depended to carry out many practical and political functions) through the upward mobility of leading members of the non-aristocratic strata. This required a radical change in how people understood their social world. The existing order was one of fixed 'estates', God-given social ranks which people were born into and could not fundamentally transcend. Large-scale social mobility was simply not possible within that theologically grounded worldview. To achieve and consolidate the inconceivable change required, the idea of the nation as a community within which all were *equal* subjects of the monarch was born. This meant that social mobility could be understood as entirely possible, and that a new basic self-respect could be felt by all deemed to be subjects.

This account is of particular interest to us here because although it fits the modernist template in seeing national feeling as an artefact which emerged to serve a socio-political purpose, it has a persuasive explanation for the depth of the nation's psychological appeal. It identifies a psychological need that is met, and benefit that is brought, by the definition of oneself as a subject or citizen who is in a fundamental respect the equal of all others in the nation. This is summed up in the concept of dignity, which we have identified as a key theme in the psychology of politics. The concept of the nation which, according to Greenfeld, crystallised in sixteenth-century England, had at its centre the principle of an irreducible individual dignity for all, irrespective of whatever inequalities, oppressions and privations may have dominated the lives of many. And, argues Greenfeld, it is this deeply attractive feature of national identity which has driven the spread of nationalism around the world, although the conditions and consequences of its uptake differ widely according to context.

Overall, Greenfeld sees national identity and its democratisation of dignity as the basis for the subsequent global development of democratic institutions. She goes on to see it also as the basis for the spread of capitalism, and for the individualism (both its freedoms and its costs) of the modern and post-modern world. But whether or not we might agree with her broader conclusions, or indeed with her specific theory of the Tudor origins of national identity, we can suggest on the basis of her work that an important element in the love of nation is — whatever particular nation we might be considering — to be found in the dignified equality of membership it can be felt to confer. This equality might exist more in principle or in hope than in reality, but as support for an inner sense of self-worth it is of major psychological value. We can therefore understand why changes in national identity, if felt to de-value the dignity it confers, can produce fearful and aggressive responses.

THE INSECURITY OF DIGNITY

Let's look at this a little more closely, and consider how the universal endowment of dignity may interact with individual differences in personal reserves of dignity. We saw in Chapter 1 that the inner foundations for robust self-respect are laid in early development. Individuals with a relatively secure, inner sense of their personal worth may appreciate their membership of a nation which appears to reflect and to strengthen that sense by recognising them as dignified citizens. But they will be able to take a critical stance towards their own nation when they think that is necessary. This is because they have sufficient personal reserves of 'dignity capital', to use Greenfeld's phrase, and so they are not seriously threatened by the (perhaps temporary) reduction of dignity which a voluntary and partial dis-identification with their nation may involve.

Individuals with a less secure sense of their personal worth may have turned to a national identity as a source of basic dignity supply, and if so any threat to that supply will be a more serious psychological challenge. Such threats may come in various forms (real and/or perceived), including internal challenges to the principle of equality, or external threats to the existence of the nation. Individuals with the least secure sense of their personal dignity may have also inflated the dignity which they believe themselves to be granted by their nationality, by aggrandising the nation and so increasing the imagined dignity value of belonging to it.

This inflation of dignity is to be found in some cases of what Vamik Volkan describes as 'chosen glories', elements of national consciousness focusing on a past historical or mythological event which symbolises the greatness of the nation. This national triumph will typically be a battle won, whether at the founding or early life of the nation or in its more recent history. The Battle of the Boyne could be seen as such an element in the British national identity of Protestants in Northern Ireland. In 1690, in what is now the Republic of Ireland, an army led by William of Orange defeated one led by the former King James II of England. The battle consolidated the joint monarchy in England of William and his wife Mary, and ensured continued Protestant domination of Ireland, and its union with England. Although developments in the twentieth century restricted the union to the northern six counties, Protestant Unionists there continue to celebrate the Battle with annual marches which have been major flashpoints in decades of tension and conflict with Catholic Republicans.

It could be argued that the World War II Battle of Britain, a period of aerial warfare across several months in 1940, became a 'chosen glory' in British national identity. Although it was early in the war, it is seen by military historians as a major setback for Nazi Germany, and by many of the British public as a demonstration of their own resilience, continued under the 'Blitz' of German bombing raids, and of the valour of their aircrews.

However, it is a matter of debate whether, in the celebration of these battles, there is an *inflation* of the dignity of the national identities concerned. May the British public not feel rightful pride at Britain's role in the defeat of Nazism, and even be allowed a little idealisation of it? How long ago may an event be before it should lose its role in defining and bestowing dignity on a present-day community, or at least fade into the background? And how much can the celebration of a glorious triumph be at odds with the historical reality of the actual event or situation?

Once we begin to look at particular examples it becomes clear that psychological evaluation inevitably becomes entangled with political and social values. How we view a 'chosen glory' mythology depends on the significance of its representation in present-day politics as well as on the extent to which it embodies the psychological processes of splitting and delusional idealisation. Present commemorations of the Battle of the Boyne involve a more desperate and divisive striving for dignity than do commemorations of the Battle of Britain, although some dim resonance of the latter may be a factor in contemporary negative British attitudes towards the rest of Europe. Given the very small margin in Britain's 'Brexit' referendum in favour of leaving the EU, that outcome could well have been determined by the need of some voters to recover or defend dignity by fending off perceived encroachments by, or attacks from, mainland Europe. If so, however, it is not the chosen glory of Battle of Britain mythology which is responsible, but the low reserves of dignity capital amongst sections of the British people, and their consequent vulnerability to an 'easy fix' of their dignity deficit which they imagined that Brexit would bring.

THE OTHER SIDE OF THE COIN: HUMILIATION

We cannot consider dignity in isolation from other states of mind to which it is connected. The deepest connections are often between opposites, so we must now turn to indignity or humiliation. (A dignity deficit can also take the form of indignancy, as recognised in the naming of the Indignados movement in Spain in 2011.) We find, perhaps surprisingly, that humiliation is a theme in much nationalist discourse. Indeed, it is in some cases at the heart of national self-consciousness. Again, Volkan (2001) has led the way into this territory, with the other side of his coin of chosen mythologies. The inverse of the chosen glory is the 'chosen trauma', a deliberate focus (if unknowingly so) on a defining experience of catastrophe, whether that is a clear matter of historical fact or a more mythological construction.

While humiliation and trauma have clearly different meanings, for our purposes here these concepts converge. Humiliation of many kinds may be traumatic for the humiliated one. Trauma of any sort usually involves vulnerability and a loss of control, and the traumas of nations typically also involve defeat, subjugation or persecution. So national trauma, whether in present reality, the distant past or mythology, is likely to evoke some sense of humiliation in the victims, and in those identified with them.

In a number of cases, the identity of a nation is tied to a chosen trauma, a mythology of defeat and humiliation, sometimes based on an event many centuries ago. One of Volkan's examples is the importance in Serbian nationalism of the Battle of Kosovo, at which, back in 1389, a Serbian army was defeated by an Ottoman force. This laid the way for Serbian territory to be completely taken into the Ottoman Empire in the fifteenth century. Volkan notes how this distant humiliation was used by Serbian leaders in the 1990s to justify the genocidal massacres of Muslims. The German experience of humiliation in the 1919 Treaty of Versailles, and its influence on the emergence of the Nazi movement, is well-documented, as is the similar Hungarian experience of the 1920 Treaty of Trianon, a grievance nurtured by fascists in the interwar period and still a powerful force in Hungarian politics today. And if 9/11 was for many Americans a traumatic demonstration of their vulnerability at home, after decades of superpower status which encouraged the experience of a kind of invulnerability, that helps to make sense of the apparent power of the rallying call to 'Make America great again' in Donald Trump's 2016 campaign for the presidency. So it is not difficult to find examples of a shared traumatic experience, or perhaps less dramatic erosions of the sense of safety and dignity, being followed, either directly or down the years, by surges of aggressive nationalism which create conflict with other nations and/or within an existing nation.

Post-colonial national liberation movements are bound to be marked by the insecurities and indignities of being colonised, and they may carry the impulse to pass those bad experiences on to others, or to return them to the colonisers – or their representatives. Post-colonial conflict in Sri Lanka has been between the majority Sinhalese and the minority of Tamils, with the latter seeking independence for the north-east region where they are concentrated. The view of many Sinhalese was that the Tamils had been preferred by the British (in educational provision, recruitment to government service and political representation), and so had contributed to the humiliation of colonisation, and this fed into the conflict that developed after independence in 1948, although that had other older and deeper roots. In the case of the Rwandan genocide of 1994, the Tutsi victims were a minority who had been preferred by the Belgian colonial power and had dominated the Hutu majority for decades – though not since a Hutu-led republic had been established in 1962. There had been a long history of conflict and savage violence between the two groups before and since 1962, with and without fomentation by European powers. So while post-colonial revenge was one long-standing factor, it seems that generations of competition and violence undermining safety and dignity on both sides had destroyed what emotional capital might once have existed to moderate the intensity of the hatreds. A fuller understanding of this atrocity would have to describe how that history had shaped the minds of the Hutu leaders who planned and organised it and those who carried it out, and why the culture and institutions of Rwandan society had been unable to contain the murderousness.

Some recent traumas are immediately present in the experience of a people, while others are still felt with some directness but have been transmitted across two or more generations. In a process whereby the children of direct victims are shaped by their experiences of traumatised parents, and their children affected in turn, a shared sense of still-active collective trauma is sustained. Israeli national identity is closely tied to the Jewish trauma of the Holocaust, and to the long history of the Jews as a persecuted and dispersed people. And of course the international attempt to repair the damage of this traumatic history has inserted a massive trauma into the heart of Palestinian identity.

Taking humiliation into account as well as dignity we can now revisit, in the context of understanding nationalisms, our general account of early psychological development. In early life we are all totally dependent on others, a situation of need and humiliation which generates extreme anxiety. In good-enough development, we are able to develop trust in our significant others, and so to tolerate the awareness of our dependence, and the anxiety and the humiliation which it involves. This acceptance of humiliation, because it is realistic and because it basically welcomes the connection with the other, paves the way to a self-experience of security and thereby of dignity. Trust in others will also be linked to an experience of the self as worthy of others' care, and so enhance self-worth. This emotional capital enables the person in adult life to tolerate situations of dependency, threat and potential humiliation.

Those with less secure self-worth and internal sense of dignity will be more susceptible to *intolerable* feelings of humiliation in a range of situations of real or perceived dependency or threat, and thus be more likely to try and defend against those feelings. This may be by reaching for a more aggrandised sense of self, including the 'national self', as noted above. Or it could be by fixating angrily on the need to avenge the humiliation, which appears to be a key factor in the case of some post-colonial nationalisms (it is also a major driver of contemporary 'Islamist terrorism', as we will see in Chapter 4).

One way or another, the relative strengths of *internal* states of dignity and humiliation, in an individual mind and in the aggregated national psyche, are important factors in determining the political profile of that individual citizen or that national public. In the dignity/humiliation dynamic as played out in national and international politics, the reckless grandiosity of some nationalisms does not stem from an excess or over-valuation of national dignity, but from an inner feeling, or fear, of humiliation – that is, from a dignity deficit.

This dynamic is a major presence in the 'ethnic' content which is at the heart of most nationalisms. However we have seen that the idea of the 'civic' is necessary to round out the content of much contemporary nationalism, by infusing it with principles (such as the rule of law and universal suffrage) which are essential to liberal democracy. This does not mean, however, that civic is the good form of nationalism and ethnic the bad. It is more a question of what kinds of feelings and ideas are involved in any particular form of nationalism – what psychological needs it meets, and what impulses or emotional resources it mobilises. We have seen how dangerous it can be when reserves of dignity capital are low in the national public. But we must also give brief consideration to some other important themes in the psychology of nationalism, and look at how they interact with the dignity/humiliation dynamic.

NARCISSISM, MERGER AND SAFETY

It is not difficult to see the imprint of narcissism in many nationalisms, especially in the extreme versions of what is now often called ethno-nationalism, that is, nationalism with an emphasis on ethnic identity in the racial sense of 'ethnic'.[3] This is a typically a visceral and angry variety, in which the nation is intensely idealised (often around parental imagery, of which more below). The intensity of connection to the nation of which national anthems often speak suggests that the nationalist citizen experiences a kind of merger, in which the self has disappeared into the national body. The psychological basis of this nationalism lies in the collective use of narcissistic defences. As we have seen, narcissism is always a defence, which in this political context may be against any humiliation, abandonment or annihilation which the nation might face.

However, individuals are likely to become involved in such collective narcissism only when they have their own personal reasons for employing its defensive functions, so the specific dynamics and objects of the defence will differ from person to person. The narcissistic investment in the nation is like a final common pathway for a host of individual anxieties, with everyone in the angry crowd turning to the idealised nation as a balm for their separate woes. The threats to the nation which they perceive are likely to be projections of the threats which (unconsciously) they feel to their own selves. In the fullest dose of the hoped-for medicine, there will be a total dedication to the cause, a merger with the nation in terms of everyday life, relationships and aspirations, as well as at the level of unconscious phantasy in which the self is identified with the body of the nation.

While other ethnic nationalisms do not necessarily involve primitive phantasies of merger, they often involve a phantasy of the nation as an ideal home: safe, trustworthy and pure. When the nation's essence is defined, wholly or partly, in terms of blood or genes, then we have an intellectual rationale for xenophobic or racist forms of nationalism. Other nations are correspondingly denigrated, even demonised, and at its most dangerous, this kind of nationalism demands that the lost purity of the nation be restored, at whatever cost to those deemed to represent the impurities. The search for purity is a search for a trustworthy object; only the pure can be trusted. As such it is an endless and hopeless task, because it is not reality-oriented. It is not driven by a scarcity of trustworthy objects, but by an anxious inability to trust, so any imagined purity that is found soon becomes untrustworthy and impure. There is always a threat of further impurity, and thus a risk that another category of people will emerge as the target of the next round of purification. (In Chapter 4 we will see this process at the heart of fascism.) In a similar way, the endless fragmentation of extremist sects is also based on this delusional, impossible search for the safety afforded by a trustable object.

THE NATION AS IMAGINED FAMILY

As we saw in Chapter 1, Volkan suggests that we all need some large-group identity as a *core* part of our selves. Not everyone would agree with this from their own experience; some people may feel that their core self is entirely defined in their interpersonal and small-group relations. So the 'core-ness' of national identity is not universal. Nonetheless, the strength of national identity for many people, and its importance in their self-definition, is often evidenced in the language and imagery associated with it. There are numerous examples of the nation's representation as a parent-figure, suggesting it is of deepest emotional significance.

The terms Fatherland and Motherland are familiar references to one's home nation, and although the words for parents do not always carry major significance when used metaphorically, in the context of national feeling it is likely that they do. Interestingly there are several examples which suggest an effort, through the words, to imagine the nation as a combined parental figure, fusing the assets of both parental genders, as in the French word 'patrie', a feminine noun based on the root of the word for 'father', which can be translated as both motherland and fatherland, as can the equivalent words in Italian, Spanish and Portuguese.

An interesting recent study[4] of national anthems revealed the major place in their lyrics of familial imagery − over half of the 200 anthems studied had some familial imagery, confirming the researchers' hypothesis that nations are better seen as 'imagined families' than as 'imagined communities'. Over one third had paternal or patrilineal imagery, compared to 12% with maternal, showing the predominance of masculinity in the gendered composition of nations. Gender-neutral and androgynous images of the nation do, however, exist, so single-gendering is not essential to the idea of nations. Sibling references are also common.

As well as being its creators, parent-nation figures are often presented as the defenders of the nation, its values and its people, e.g. in artistic representations of the mother-figure as warrior or formidable authority. At the same time, the language and imagery of parental symbolism may evoke a desire amongst citizens to protect the parent-nation. This can be a very powerful impulse, based on gratitude felt towards the parents who have given us life and protection, and also on guilt relating to the anger and envy which all children have felt towards their parents, as we saw in Chapter 1. There could also be an element of fearful intimidation by such overwhelmingly powerful figures. (The 85-metre high statue in Volgograd of the Motherland calling, sword in hand, would seem to invite a measure of fear, as at one time the imposing figure of Britannia with long trident and shield might perhaps have done.)

The protective impulse obviously can be exploited by propaganda of various sorts, especially insofar as it is driven by guilt, which is more likely to be unconscious, and therefore undermanaged. Not only propaganda to drive up a war effort, but appeals to rise up against any others seen as destroying the nation, as portrayed in much contemporary populism, may be well-received by minds anxious to preserve or repair relationships with parent-figures in relation to whom much guilt is felt as a legacy of the aggression felt towards them in earlier development.

This brings us again to the toxicity of nationalism. To its cosmopolitan opponents, the danger of national feeling is nowhere more clear than when it comes dressed up in parental imagery. The association of this imagery with Nazism, the irrationality of equating something as huge and complex as a nation with a parent, the unhealthy mix of adoration, submissiveness and belligerence which often surrounds such imagery, all point to the sick heart of nationalism as perceived by its many critics. And indeed these are serious points.

THE NATION AS SAFE CONTAINER VS. THE 'SECURITY STATE'

However, that is not all there is to be said about the nation as parent or family. That imagery may now belong to previous centuries (except perhaps in national anthems); it is arguably part of a largely departed culture of deference and melodrama. However, it lingers, and we need to evaluate it as a more complex phenomenon than the critique of it allows. While family is for some an image of patriarchy, or claustrophobia, in reality it is the place where most of us come from, and to which we owe a lot of our emotional capital as well as our problems. To symbolise one's nation as a family could therefore be an expression of gratitude towards the society in which one has been nurtured, and a commitment to reproduce its provision of care and protection. It is also an acknowledgment of a dependency need, and carries a hope, an expectation even, that the need can be met by a 'containing object'.

As we have seen, containment is a fundamental process on which sanity and society depend. In its purest and strongest form, containment is a process between two people – which initially means a caregiver and an infant. The one acknowledges the anxieties and other difficult feelings of the other, and conveys that they can be faced, and survived. A parent figure is thus the prototypical containing object, but later in life we can find containment in cultural experiences which offer opportunities to confront threatening feelings (via music, art, sport, etc.) while demonstrating to us that they can be tolerated and managed. The projection of parental imagery onto an object such as a 'nation' suggests that it is felt, or hoped, to have containing power.

This power of the nation rests in part on its symbolisation as home, the place where we come from and where we can find some kind of safety, however rudimentary. While physical security cannot readily be expected in many nations, at the symbolic level there is a measure of safety in familiarity. Despite the globalisation of consumer goods, there are still national specificities in food and other aspects of material culture, such as vernacular architecture. So our daily experiences of food and shelter arrive through the medium of national culture. This is a statement of the obvious, yet its psychological implications can be ignored. Language is usually a key component of national identity, because the sound of the 'mother' tongue is an important element in an experience of enfolding familiarity. (For the same reason, language is often a fault-line of intra-national differentiation and conflict within bi-lingual nations such as Canada and Belgium.) Familiarity can be containing not only because we recognise things around us, and thus can experience them as containing objects, but also because we are can anticipate *being* recognised and accepted by them.

In its role as the fundamental unit of government, the nation is able to gather to itself additional sources of containing capacity. Even in a neo-liberal world, the nation-*state* is the ultimate protector and provider for its citizens, so is in a material sense the heir to parental authority and responsibility. In its provision of public utilities, health care and welfare (insofar as it takes responsibility for these), it offers material responses to anxieties concerning illness, incapacity and death. The state is probably the closest match of any institution to the parental matrix (as we used that term in Chapter 1), in that it incorporates all the core parental functions of providing for, protecting and restraining and guiding the behaviours of its charges.[5]

ANTIPATHIES TOWARDS THE NATION-STATE

So except in those cases where a self-identified nation is not a state, our attachments to nations are closely linked to our dependencies on states. However, the state is the institutionalisation of leadership, and so we have as deep an ambivalence towards the state as we do towards leaders. Like many ambivalences, this is typically managed by a division of emotional labour. Some people in a society spring to the attack, while others leap to the defence. The most full-frontal attack on the state has come from 'neo-liberalism', which we will look at more closely in the next chapter, and focusses on a critique of the state as the antithesis of freedom, especially the freedom for markets to operate without restraint. However, libertarianisms of the Left and the centre have also contributed substantially to spreading suspicion of the state, for example, in opposition to what they see as a sinisterly encroaching 'security state' which wants to establish regimes of surveillance and control over all its citizens. Proposals for identity cards, where these don't already exist, and the introduction of counter-terrorism intelligence gathering, are foci for libertarian protest, while security leaks and 'whistle-blowing' are applauded. In the UK, the government's counter-terrorism programme 'Prevent' has been the object of particular hostility as an intrusive 'snooper's charter'. It is ironic that for some people 'security' now connotes the opposite of its literal meaning, in that 'securitisation', for example, refers to extensions of the state's reach which are believed to put the freedom and privacy of citizens at risk.

As well as fears of intrusion, the spectre of corruption is an important component in many people's perceptions of the state, and one that is becoming more common in the established liberal democracies where until recently the lack of trust in politics focussed mainly on charges of incompetence, infighting and duplicity. For example, in 2009 there was an outbreak across the UK of huge opprobrium directed towards the chief political representatives of the UK state, Members of Parliament, when some were found to have used their expense accounts to pay for personal purchases which should not have been covered by public funds. The amounts involved were trivial compared to the bonuses which many people in the private sector have been receiving for years, but the dishonesty of the payments led to sustained moral outrage.

So the nation-state, and the ideas of 'the government' or 'politicians' or 'the establishment' with which it may be conflated, are somewhat short of friends at the moment, and under attack from various directions, at least in the liberal democracies. It could even be suggested that a *hatred* of the state has become normative across the West. There certainly is an ambivalence towards the nation-state, which is the source of much tension and conflict within societies. Psychologically, however, we find it easier to line ourselves up on one side or the other, for or against the nation or the nation-state, than to experience the ambivalence within ourselves, since that brings all the discomforts of uncertainty and inner conflict. Turning our internal ambivalences into external conflicts is often more comfortable.

But in principle, the nation or the nation-state can be a 'good object' for its citizens – a realistic one, not grossly idealised, which can meet needs for a sense of dignity, home and safety. Accordingly, a benign nationalism, in the sense of a positive view of one's nation, a wish for its continuation and a desire to contribute to it, coupled with equal respect for other nations, should be possible. Still, any attempt to reach an optimistic conclusion here has to be qualified. While we should not underestimate the presence of nationalist feeling of that sort in many countries today, it cannot be said that benign nationalism is a dominant force in the world.

Building on earlier discussion in this chapter, we can identify two reasons for this. Firstly, it has been discredited and displaced by virulent forms of ethno-nationalism, which feed off the increasing inequalities across the world (to be examined later), and the depletion of dignity capital and other forms of emotional capital. Aggressive and divisive ethno-nationalisms are not caused by the search for dignity and safety through national identity; the problem is rather in the perversion of that search by the strength of other factors: the intensity of the inner sense of humiliation, of fears of abandonment, or of terrifying phantasies of annihilation. These can dictate the terms of the search, and result in narcissistic and other defensive forms of nationalism emerging.

Secondly, benign nationalism is stymied in its development by the weakness of the most basic condition for its development: that the nation-state can be experienced as a familiar and safe home. For many people the pace of social change, and the level of social tensions (where again rising inequalities are partly responsible), are such that the nation is not always seen as a strong force in the world, nor as a coherent object, a recognisable and effective moral community which can offer some containment.

4

IDEOLOGIES

THE CORE PSYCHOLOGICAL QUESTION

Ideology is sometimes seen as the main root of political evil. Especially in classical liberal views of the world, an ideology is a rigid and toxic set of ideas, with the power to command the minds, and the behaviours, of those people who for some reason are enthralled by it. It is based on falsehoods, though ones which are passionately believed, so it is in the realm of delusion or illusion rather than lies or corruption. As such it is frequently intertwined with naïve and missionary forms of idealism; it typically claims to be showing the way to a better world.

Marxist theory offered a different use of the term. It proposed that our ideas about the social world and how it works are determined by our place in society. As such, they always embody ideology: they tend to reflect the outlook and interests of the social class to which we belong. This is not a relativist view, for which ideologies are expressions of different points of view, and all could be at least partly true. It sees proletarian ideology as the only correct one, because the working class are in a position to understand that capitalism is both exploitative and unsustainable. Bourgeois ideology is set of self-serving illusions about the system clung to by those who benefit from it.[1]

While both of these approaches now seem dated, they continue to influence some political debates, in that opponents' ideas may be dismissed as 'ideology', or as the wrong ideology. We will use the term 'ideology' here in a broad and neutral way, to mean any set of ideas which purport to explain key features of society, to advocate certain principles or policies derived from those ideas, and thereby to shape political behaviour. On this definition, most people have got some sort of ideology.

The best known and most impactful ideologies have mostly been '-isms', such as socialism and fascism. Nationalism is often seen as an ideology, though in itself it does not have any specific ideas or political content beyond the assertion of the nation. Similarly, 'authoritarianism' may be very important politically, but can be linked to a wide range of political agendas and programmes. Neo-liberalism and Islamism are frequently referenced in discussions of politics today, and both have abundant political content, though both are confusingly named, particularly 'Islamism', which has little or no intrinsic relationship to the religion of Islam.

Ideology and ideologies have been much studied in the social science disciplines, which overlap with ideologies, since both are concerned with explaining society. Knowledge of how and where an ideology has developed, which groups have taken it up, with what consequences – all that is important in understanding its place in the world today. The core psychological question about any ideology is about its appeal: what attracts people to vote for it, promote it, march for it, perhaps to become violent in its service. And why does it appeal to some people and not to others who might seem to have the same reasons for supporting it? In its study of ideology, much political psychology has tended towards *socialisation* approaches to those questions – that is to say, it has placed the emphasis on the individual's environment and the social influences to which we have been exposed, family and peer group pressures, the opportunities to become involved with particular groups or movements, etc. While these factors must all be examined, this type of approach risks missing the *internal* drivers of political outlook and action – which should be the core target of *psychological* inquiry.

The main idea offered in this chapter is that we can 'read' an ideology as a state of mind, as an expression of feelings or of phantasy (as we defined that term in Chapter 1). We can then understand its appeal to those individuals who take it up: it reflects and validates their own states of mind, and affords some expression of feelings (which may or may not also have other expression in their lives). The states of mind in question could be based on powerful unconscious phantasy, a legacy of early emotional development, and if so the individual's relationship to the ideology will be intense. Seeing ideology this way enables us to explain why particular individuals are drawn to particular ideologies. The pathways of emotional development are varied, and even within close communities can produce a range of outcomes in the emotional lives and characters of the adults who as children shared the same social environment. Thus we have the possibility of explaining why one person becomes a centrist politician while someone from the same street with a very similar socio-cultural background becomes a violent extremist.

Notably, this variability within communities is probably increasing as social cohesion diminishes under pressure from globalisation, and neighbours vary more in the cultural and emotional legacies they inherit.

NEO-LIBERALISM

At the centre of most ideologies is a statement of something which is good, and a complementary identification of something which is bad. An ideology consists, essentially, of a set of ideas in which the good object is praised, and the bad object is criticised. The term 'neo-liberalism' has become ever more widely and loosely used, but we will employ it here in the hope that it does still denote a meaningful phenomenon: a political standpoint or philosophy in which the central principle is that free markets should be the basis of human society, from which follow prescriptions about, at the least, economic management, with other areas of life – welfare, education, security, culture, etc. – probably also seen as needing to be more fully organised along the lines of marketisation.

It is clear what the central good object is here: a concept of the free market. In the writings of the twentieth-century economist Friedrich Hayek (1944), an unregulated market was seen not only as the best basis for economic life but also as embodying an ideal vision of free individuals able to act independently and make their own choices in life. This vision of a good society as one comprising sovereign individuals (sometimes seen as acting with or on behalf of their families) is at the heart of most varieties of contemporary 'neo-liberalism'. The competitiveness which markets engender is typically seen from this standpoint in simply positive terms, as the driver of efficiency. The major inequalities of market-based societies are accepted, either on meritocratic grounds ('ability and/or hard work bring just reward') or on a sub-Darwinian assumption of their inevitability ('that's life').

This idealisation of the free market is inextricably linked with a damnation of the state and all its works. The state is basically a threat to the liberty of the individual; while claiming to act in the general interest it imposes damaging restrictions on markets and individuals, depriving them of choice and making oppressive demands via taxation and bureaucracy. It also encourages dependency and greed amongst weaker citizens.

This last point is a clue to the psychological meaning of the ideology. If we consider neo-liberalism as a state of mind, what stands out firstly is the denial of dependency. The unfettered individual of the neo-liberal imagination has no dependency needs. S/he wants to be free to act in the autonomous pursuit of self-interest, to which all relationships with others are secondary, and s/he has little or no responsibility for those people who need support in life. Human society is not a network of interdependencies, but a fortunate aggregation of freely acting individuals/families.

In psychological terms, this insistence on the independence and self-sufficiency of the individual is a narcissistic defence against dependency, and as such it can deliver an experience of both safety and dignity, albeit in false form. (The psychic benefits arising from the use of any defence are very likely to be false, since the defence is built on an untruth.) The illusion of self-sufficiency can produce the illusion of safety, as there is no need for risky dependence on others. And a measure of dignity may be found in the image of the proud individuals who are able to take responsibility for themselves and to thrive in the marketplaces of life. In the middle of the last century the psychoanalyst Erich Fromm had captured much of this tragically shrunken and lonely mode of experiencing the world, in his concept of the 'amoral marketing orientation'.[2] The political philosopher C.B. Macpherson's concept of 'possessive individualism' emphasised how the cornerstone of this view of the world was the idea that we are the inalienable owners of ourselves, and owe nothing to society for this ownership. 'Society consists of relations of exchange between proprietors',[3] beyond which we have no obligations to others.

As we saw in Chapter 1, a narcissistic defence is likely to become a significant part of the adult character when in earlier life the capacity to tolerate dependency could not develop, because it was difficult or impossible to achieve a trusting relationship with a caregiver. Another legacy of that situation is likely to be a reserve of deeply negative feeling towards parent-figures. We have also seen how in adult life the state takes on a sort of *in loco parentis* role in the public uncon-scious. It therefore makes psychological sense that, in the realm of ideology, a narcissistic idealisation of the marketised world of free and independent individuals will be coupled with a suspicious and resentful attitude towards the state. Critiques of the state as remote and self-serving, or as intrusive and domineering, may or may not reflect aspects of the actual state in the real world, but they can cer-tainly draw on memories or phantasies of parents who did not meet the child's needs.

The unconscious template of an uncaring or oppressive parent can be made even more toxic by the addition of an element of sibling rivalry. There is presently an important convergence between the neo-liberal rejection of the state and the perceptions of sections of the public who in other respects can be much more positive about the state, and negative about markets. This convergence is seen in hostile working-class views about the state's indulgence of so-called work-shy citizens, its weakness in tackling benefit fraud, and its excessive generosity towards immigrants, at the expense of the nonimmigrant population. The villainous figure of the parent who neglects their own child yet provides for other children, or perversely favours the least deserving amongst its own, is the psychological source of some of the rage around the state's allocation of housing and benefits.

This critique of neo-liberal ideology does not uniquely patholo-gise its proponents. A measure of discomfort around dependency is common enough, and there are other ways of dealing with it apart from converting it into a political outlook. So neo-liberalism is not alone in the psychological defence it expresses or draws upon. Nor does our critique demolish it intellectually, or invalidate it as a politi-cal project. There are important and complex issues around the nature of markets and their relationship to the state, which obviously can-not be condensed into psychological analysis. The value of psycho-logical work of this kind is that it offers a way of understanding the emotional needs and the defences which people bring to the table of politics. This is especially important when we do so in such a way that the emotional dimension then becomes the predominant one in determining our opinions and actions. And even when that is not the case, to have some insight into the links between our politics and our more hidden selves should nudge us towards a more thoughtful political discourse.

COMMUNISM

While neo-liberalism as we know it did not emerge until the second half of the twentieth century, the ideology of which it is the clearest 'opposite' was already on the wane by then, though it still exerts some influence today – the ideology of communism. In the communist countries of the twentieth century, the state was, in its fusion with the Communist Party, a massively revered parental object, at least in official ideology – more ambivalent relationships with the state must have prevailed in many people's minds. State control of the economy did, of course, mean that the state was a provider, with fully socialised health and welfare systems able to underwrite at least rudimentary levels of care, and therefore of at least some measure of both safety and dignity. Especially when life experience has not been reassuring about the reliability of other people, the impersonal state may seem a safer option, if only at the level of ideology and policy (when it comes to actual care, we all seek a personal 'human' touch). And the possibility of being part of a glorious story of deeply shared societal advancement is a powerful dignity developer. Even in the 2011–2015 Five Year Plan of the Communist Party of China, reflecting as it does this present era of deep marketisation and widespread corruption, there is affirmation of the principle of unity in one set of ideas, and the primacy of Party and state: 'we should hold high the great banner of socialism with Chinese characteristics. Under the guidance of Deng Xiaoping Theory and the important thought of Three Represents'. The 'Three Represents' is a doctrine continuous with Mao Zedong Thought, i.e. the 'masses' and the 'people' are the objects with which it is imperative to merge oneself. The doctrine demands that:

> 'Party officials, especially leaders at all levels, must be incorruptible and self-disciplined and share weal and woe with the masses. At all times and under any circumstances, Party officials must follow the Party's mass line, adhere to the objective of serving the people wholeheartedly, and take benefiting the people as the starting and end points of all their work'.[4]

The 'people' is a monolithic object of worship. Similarly, traditional western communist positioning of working-class people as all brothers and sisters to each other points to an element of idealised sibling relationships in the picture of class 'solidarity', a term which carries a resonance of being fused with the revered collective. Words and images which suggest these kinds of merger should ring warning bells; they point to a regressive wish to lose the self in the imagined safety and strength of the perfect collective, built around an omnipotent parent.

Here we have one example of an issue which arises repeatedly in trying to understand the psychology of politics. This critical analysis of the term 'solidarity' must not be taken to delete other things which can be said about it. 'Solidarity' with others need not convey a regressive impulse, but a genuinely selfless commitment to the legitimate interests and well-being of others in one's group. In pointing to the possible unconscious meanings of our actions, we are not saying that the political and moral reasons people may have for acting as they do are *always* superficial rationalisations concealing the unconscious needs which are the real drivers of behaviour. In the complexities of human behaviour, moral principle and unconscious need may act side by side. Indeed, the capacity to act in a principled way is as much based on inner psychic life as is the capacity to act in selfish or destructive ways. What is crucial is the strength of the secure and realistic parts of the psyche relative to that of the insecure and defensive parts, and the prospects for strengthening the former and containing the latter.

So insofar as communist ideology has been seen by some as an idealistic vision of a good parent/state protecting and respecting its citizens, it is not difficult to understand its appeal. However, in the Stalinist realities of communism in practice, the safety on offer came to be conditional upon conformity or quiescence, with a consequent erosion of dignity. But the regime persisted, supported as massive orthodoxies often are, not only by coercive means but psychologically by splitting. For every idealised good object there is always a 'bad object', sometimes hidden, sometimes dominant. Once communism came to power, the bad object was divided into two: the capitalist enemy without, and the enemy within, manifest in deviation and disloyalty.

Still, amongst the conforming there remained some genuine belief in the ideology, in the experience of full identification with an image of the state as an omnipotent, idealised parent, who knows what is best and must be obeyed. And despite the wide dissolution of such attitudes across the former 'communist bloc', there is continuing influence of socialist ideologies in the twenty-first century, which, when psychologically understood, suggest a phantasy of a good parent emerging and taking beneficent charge of things.

FASCISM

Interestingly, that could also be a description of the state of mind expressed in fascist ideology. There, the longed-for ideal object is once again linked to the state, although in fascism there is typically a charismatic leader into whose persona the state (and party) is absorbed, as is also the case in some communist examples, such as Mao Zedong or the Kim dynasty. In his merger with the state (whether there could be a *female* fascist leader is an important question we will touch on shortly), the leader is mandated by the people to use the power of the state to protect them and to make them strong. (The term 'fascism' is derived from the Latin word *fasces*, bundles of sticks with an axe projecting which were carried into the Roman court by officials to represent the authority of the state.) The glorified, omnipotent leader/state is a perversion of a protective father. The 'goodness' of the fascist leader is an illusion based on splitting, but is seen by some to offer a promise of safety in membership of the societal family.

So acute is the fear that even this family may not be safe that it has to be defined in very restrictive terms, to keep out all possible sources of threat. All totalitarian mindsets are sustained by a vision of safety in purity. Potentially overwhelming anxieties about contamination, collapse or some other threat to the self are managed by projecting the threat into others who must then be kicked out or kept out of the family. Even then, they can remain a threat, and so the need for a final solution. While fascism has its enemies within its own camp, its construction of an *external* bad object which must be annihilated is one of the most extreme and destructive states of political mind, though as other genocides show, this catastrophic phenomenon can also develop without much of the rationalisation which an ideology provides. 'External' in this context does not necessarily mean physically outside of a national boundary; in the anti-semitism, apparent homophobia and hatred for groups (such as the Roma) often associated with fascist and neo-fascist groups, the enemy is very much within the fascist's community, though 'outside' of the group defined as 'us'.

Overall we can therefore see how a deeply anxious state of mind may be vulnerable to fascist propaganda. Another point to note about the psychology of fascism is the likely role that sexuality and gender play in its development. The hatred of women in Nazism, and the Nazis' preoccupations with perverse sexual fantasies, are well-documented.[5] The fascistic hatred of weakness and dependency can be seen as part of a desperate hyper-masculinisation which is staving off fears of a collapse of the masculine self. The possibility of a female fascist leader is therefore small, unless it was a woman who could save the fascist male self by somehow donating to it the experience of invincible power.

VIOLENT TAKFIRI ISLAMISM

Our next example is remarkably similar to fascism in its psychological base. The form of political violence which has emerged in recent decades and rapidly become the major security threat in many parts of the world has no single source and may be hard to understand in its apparent randomness and meaninglessness. This, of course, is international terrorism, which at present we know mainly though not exclusively in its 'Islamist' variety. Actually we should not call it 'Islamist', unless we add some qualifying adjective such as 'takfiri' to indicate the connection with a very regressive, dogmatic form of Islam. Even then, the link with the religion of Islam is contentious. Certainly, the connection of terrorism to religion in the sense of spirituality is very limited. Islamist terror has connections with subcultures in Muslim communities, because that is where most of its purveyors and supporters come from. But there is no evidence that terror in the name of Allah is committed as the result of a spiritual experience of any sort, let alone a specifically Islamic one, nor as the outcome of studying Islamic texts.

For most people, it is barely comprehensible that such a creed could attract as many people as it has done, and continues to do, across the world. However, we can get closer to an understanding of its appeal if we analyse it as an ideology reflecting a state of mind. If we can get beyond the fear and loathing which it inevitably produces in us, we can see that it gives voice to an overwhelmingly fearful condition.

The appeal of 'Islamist' ideology rests on two psychological foundations. The first is an internal state of great fear. The terrorist does not feel at all safe, and the infliction of terror on others is an attempt to prevent the terrorist's own self being consumed by terror. At the core of this state of mind is a fear of punishment, not in a reality-oriented way as the consequence of something which the individual has actually done that is wrong, but as a background state of mind rooted in unconscious phantasy. The phantasy is of a brutal and infinitely powerful superego figure, which is constantly seeking absolute obedience and is ready to punish savagely any deviation.

In their exhortations to potential recruits, and to each other, Islamist terrorists refer constantly to the absolute necessity of obeying the will of Allah. The rewards of doing so are unending, as are the punishments for not doing so. Their Allah is a monstrous god who insists on the annihilation of all non-Muslims, and who provides, where it may be useful to do so, for this to be preceded by their subjection to unspeakable torture. The category of non-Muslims includes those many Muslims who takfiri Islamists do not recognize as 'real' Muslims (because they do not accept the terrorists' primitive definition of Islam), so simple profession of faith is not enough. Safety can be found only by obeying those who say that Allah demands this commitment to the violent creation of the global caliphate, since any Muslims who object that this is not Allah's will cannot be real Muslims. Anyone listening to those dissenting voices will be booking their own passage to hell.

You do not have to be a psychologist to think that anyone who joins a group based on this ideology must feel angry and estranged from the world around them, and must have some kind of impulse towards violence. Again, though, there are many ways in which such feelings can be expressed, most of which would not require the person to subjugate themselves to the boundless power of a terrible god. This subjugation is the specific psychological feature of this kind of terrorism, which in many other respects is very similar to criminal gang membership or, in some cases, to non-ideological mass killings (as in school and college shootings). Complying with Allah's wishes enables the recruit to feel safe. This is a psychic defence, one which psychoanalysis has called 'identification with the aggressor'. It explains why the bullied child becomes a bully; it is as if there are only two ways of being in the world. Either you are bullied, or you are the bully. So you take on the aggressor role in order to escape from being attacked. The escape for the individual here is to merge the self into the merciless superego, and to do its work by trying to eliminate the 'kuffar' (non-Muslims) and all apostate Muslims.

This does not require the presence of an actual external aggressor. A person can feel threatened or persecuted by her or his superego, that agency of the mind in which our capacity for moral judgment resides. As we have seen, our superegos are based primarily on our identifications with the authorities which are present in our early lives – primarily caregivers but also other adults, and cultural and social forces in the wider environment. In 'good enough' development, the superego can take the form of a loving and protective presence in the mind, as well as sometimes being a frustrating and judgmental one. But in the absence of secure identifications with trustworthy 'good objects', the cruel and vengeful superego can become a dominant force in the make-up of the individual. When projected into the world outside the individual, it can create the experience of a savage god, and drive someone into an active identification with its mercilessness.

The second psychological foundation of Islamist terror is an intense identification with other Muslims, particularly those who, it is believed, have been the victims of 'kuffar' hostility to Islam. This leads to the proud claim of revenge for past victims, and the protection of potential future ones, by attacking the kuffar world. The specific reasons for this identification may differ between individuals, depending on their personality and their social context, but they seem to stem from an internal sense of victimhood and humiliation, which is then projected onto an abstract idea of 'the Muslims', and which can be transcended through the heroic act of revenge. The lack of any authentic connection with the actual community of Muslims is reflected in the number of Muslim victims of Islamist terror, and in the way that the terrorist ideology reserves the right to decide who are 'real' Muslims and who are not.[6]

It may still be hard to understand how someone could go through these mental convolutions on the path to murder, but 'the heart has its reasons', and we must try to understand them – otherwise we are faced with an incomprehensible evil, or an inexplicable reversion to barbarism. While Islamist terror is easily seen as barbaric, it is also a modern phenomenon, as the philosopher John Gray has argued.[7] Psychologically, it must be seen as both. Its sometimes slick promotion via social and online media, its global recruitment strategies, and its calculations of effect in a mediatised world, are the works of a contemporary organisation and a 'postmodern' outlook. Yet its medieval combination of sadism and self-righteousness is regressive, both psychologically and societally. It involves the return of a pre-modern superego, and a degree of unravelling of the 'civilising process' as the sociologist Norbert Elias called it,[8] which has gradually pacified human society over the ages.

POLITICAL VIOLENCE AND PSYCHOLOGICAL DAMAGE

This analysis of the ideology of violent takfiri Islam finds it to reflect a state of mind dominated by a fearsome, primitive superego. This superego is projected out, onto the image of Allah who must be obeyed. While it is true that a skewed reading of Islamic texts can claim to furnish evidence of the existence of such a brutal god, the driver within the individual to subject the self to that god is not the Islamic text, but the individual's unforgiving, punishing superego. And to produce a violent terrorist there must also be, as we noted earlier, some impulse to violence, which allies itself with the theologised superego, so that defending the god and the *ummah*, imagined as a global community of Muslim siblings, becomes an excuse for murder.

The connection with Islam is that Islamic texts are used, very selectively, to elicit and justify the violence demanded of recruits by the terrorist groups they have joined. But this could not happen without those recruits being in states of mind that were hospitable to terror, that were actually in need of an external system of ideas or code of behaviour that could offer some safety and dignity by turning the terror onto others and making a hero of the recruit. This is the underlying need common to terrorists of very different ideologies. The perpetrators of the two most deadly attacks in the West by 'extreme right wing' terrorists, Timothy McVeigh (Oklahoma City, 1995) and Anders Breivik (Oslo and Utoya, 2011), shared with Islamists the same preoccupations with purity and punishment (as revenge and as warning to others) against a backcloth of what they saw as an epic struggle for national or world domination. The overall phenomenon of 'international terrorism' is ideologically diverse but psychologically has key features common to most cases, around the intensive use of splitting and the strength of paranoid and omnipotent phantasies. This suggests that this type of violence is the product of a convergence or intersection between certain ideologies and certain types of psychopathology. Damaged individuals, who are vulnerable perhaps to many kinds of lies and delusions, come into contact with particular lies and delusions organised as an ideology, which promises them redemption from their pains through a cathartic attack on the world, and the acquisition of hero status within a wonderful community. The political purpose of the terrorist activity is typically imprecise and distant compared with the powerful personal benefits which are imagined.

The internet has obviously facilitated this toxic intersection between personal unwellness and violent political extremism. The scope for the conversion of psychological disturbance into politicised violence was severely restricted when it depended on word-of-mouth and the circulation of books and documents. Now, it is a global trend generating 'lone actor' terrorists and people willing to act on behalf of terrorist organisations, or to join their existing operations, as in the international recruitment to the Islamic State.

One practical implication of this is that there is, or should be, a strong mental health element in counter-terrorism work. National counter-terrorism strategies such as the UK's Prevent recognise this in principle, though there is little or no elaboration of how that might be best realised in practice. Or, to look at it from a longer-term, more preventive angle, there is a counter-terrorism element in mental health work, especially the work that is focussed on children and families, in that therapeutic help brought to a child or young person struggling with insecurity and rage may help to prevent potentially violent impulses being given political expression later on – or pseudo-political as we should call it in those (many?) cases where a personal catastrophic deficit in safety and/or dignity is more important as a driver of the violence than any external world situation.

Fortunately, not all those drawn towards violent groups are actually going to be violent. Any one ideological destination may be reached by a variety of different routes through personal psychological development, since the ideology may have several different points of emotional entry. Some recruits may focus on the utopian visions which the ideology presents as the ultimate goal; others may be more enthused by the idea of an apocalyptic and violent struggle with the existing order. A psychologically diverse collection of individuals may therefore find themselves united for a while under the same ideological banner. However over time their different internal relationships to the ideology may be a source of political differences. In the decades of the 1960 and 1970s, Marxist and neo-Marxist ideology influenced many millions of people world-wide in very different situations, and for varying reasons. The political trajectories of those people in the subsequent decades varied considerably, suggesting that they had different psychological profiles underlying their earlier involvements in Marxism which subsequently put them on different paths. The person who has internalised some realistic, good-enough parental and authority figures, and so has some internal reservoir of safety and dignity, may be more tolerant of complexity and limitations in the pursuit of political goals than someone for whom the ideology represents a longed-for good experience which they have known only in phantasy, and which must be grasped by any means if it is ever to be attained.

THE VIOLENCE OF IDEALISM

Whereas classical communism found its idealised 'good object' in the totalitarian state, the ideologies of socialism when it is an insurgent force within capitalist societies find a 'bad object' in the allegedly totalitarian system of international capital from which they demand freedom. The 'good object' in an ideology of opposition to the status quo must be less concrete, more a product of the imagination, which opens up a very wide range of possible formulations of the political objective. And if we look at the ideologies of many such groups, we find something of wider importance in the psychological analysis of ideology: the appeal of an ideology can be enhanced by the ease with which it can give expression both to idealisation, as in idealistic values, and to destructive impulses, as in the sanctioning of violence to achieve the ideals and in the perversion of the ideals themselves.

This concerns a state of mind to which a regressive part of our unconscious constantly pulls us: having the cake *and* eating it. We can enjoy an idealistic fervour, and feel morally superior, while also giving ourselves permission to vent our destructive anger. Aggression becomes the righteous pursuit of justice. A simple theory of the need to destroy the existing order can legitimise the acting out of violent impulses towards diverse authorities.[9]

Such legitimations often involve a theme of major importance in many political conflicts, and one by no means restricted to the ideologies of the 'Left', that of victimhood. As in most populisms, a poorly defined 'people' are presented as the victims of the system, and the violence of riots is justified as initiating the liberation of this 'people'. An in-depth psychological analysis is not necessary for us to see the arrogance of this 'vanguardist' approach: the activist is a self-appointed saviour of the people. But with a psychological focus we might also note that in these ideologies the sense of moral superiority is strengthened by the identification with a victimised group. Once again we see the importance of a rhetoric of victims and victimhood.

LIBERAL DEMOCRACY

Let us turn now to the ideology which those of us living in liberal democracies may not spontaneously think of as an 'ideology', because it is our 'common sense', a set of principles which we often take for granted as defining the best kind of society. If we take the same approach to it as we have done to the various '-isms', will we arrive at the same sort of critique, the same exposure of the defences and perversions to be seen in the state of mind which the ideology expresses? To some extent, the answer is yes. One feature of this ideology is its tendency to underplay the more destructive sides of human nature, a tendency which can amount to denial, a defensive refusal to acknowledge the extent to which antagonisms can develop or persist even in situations where there is no external reason for them to do so. The internal drivers of negativity and conflict sit uneasily in the more rationalistic versions of liberal democratic thought, for which the continuation of tensions around religious and ethnic differences in basically free and democratic societies is hard to explain.

We might also detect a measure of narcissism in the individualistic tone of some strains of this ideology (which, like the other major ideological formations we have discussed, is actually a broad collection of different positions). Liberalism can offer space to neo-liberal refusals of collective responsibility, although this might be attenuated or partially displaced by genuine concern for others and by an accompanying rhetoric of 'one society', as in the philosophy of the 'one nation' mainstream of the Conservative Party in the UK and similar parties in other countries. Overall, insofar as it merges on one of its sides with neo-liberalism, the liberal democratic outlook should attract the same psychological (and political) critique as applied to its – misleadingly named – 'neo' offshoot.

It may also, on its 'social democratic' side, show a mild version of the idealisation of the state we have noted in socialist ideology. In the UK, the most stable feature of public opinion since regular intensive polling began in the 1970s has been the idealisation of the National Health Service (NHS). We could see it as a kind of 'chosen glory' in British political culture. This has persisted despite severe cuts to its resourcing, and despite many occasions when evidence has emerged of the presence within it of professional malpractice, incompetence and bad management. The basic principle of 'cradle to grave' care for all continues to be for many people the touchstone of good politics, a transcendent value represented on earth by the NHS and by other socialised systems of health care. The flaws of such systems are more likely to be attributed to inadequate resourcing than to the fallibility or quality of some of their staff. Even politicians of neo-liberal leanings subscribe to the NHS ideal (out of electoral necessity if not personal commitment), overlooking that despite the deep inroads of marketisation, it is governments which fund and manage systems like the NHS, and it continues to be a branch of the state.

So idealisation does occur in liberal democratic ideologies, whether the idealised object is society itself in its natural harmony, the health service for all which it supports, or perhaps some aspect of democratic process or its institutions. Just as the analysis of political ideas finds a kind of idealism in most ideologies, so a psychological analysis of ideology finds a measure of idealisation in all.

However these objections to some variants of liberal democratic ideology can be raised from within other variants of the same broad ideology. In some theories of liberal democracy, the inevitability of conflict and the importance of community are basic principles, and the liberal democratic polity is identified as the most effective frame-work for the containment of human quarrelsomeness, and for the assertion of human community and everyone's responsibility to it. These variants suggest that in particular form(s), liberal democracy could emerge from our psychological analysis with a much more positive evaluation than the others we have discussed.

Key to this is the question of splitting and the related processes of projection and idealisation. Liberal democracy can avoid the process of splitting because it does not demand belief in a perfectible world or in the realisability of ideal institutions. It can own its bad parts, and so does not have to project them and see them elsewhere. It does not need to restore the purity of a lost past, nor to create a new utopia, as it knows these cannot exist.

Many readers might object at this point. Do the preceding paragraphs not reveal the inherent bias of the approach taken here? Surely this is not objective science, when someone with a commitment to liberal democracy employs a psychological analysis which finds in favour of their own ideological position? And more specifically, is not the psychoanalytic school of psychology, drawn on here, very much a part of European intellectual traditions and so genetically related to the dominant ideology of Western democracy?

There is only one way of answering this challenge, which is to state that if psychology is a 'science', it is a moral one, and that in studying the psychology of politics we are bound to make moral and political judgments. If ideologies can be read as states of mind, then they can be analysed in terms of how they express different modes of being in the world and of relating to the people in it, modes which have different moral qualities.

Furthermore, we can also reaffirm the principle that our basic psychological needs are universally shared, and that whether or not an approach can be described as 'Eurocentric', 'Western' or 'Orientalist' is less important than whether it has succeeded in throwing some light on how these needs are responded to in different political contexts. (The same would go for approaches which might be described as 'Afrocentric' or 'Occidentalist'.) Of course, some people would say that the concept of psychological universals is itself a creation of a Western ideology which sees the rest of the world in its own image.

The important debate around this question continues, though not in this book.

In any case, it is not as if a psychological judgment in favour of liberal democracy is the end of the matter. It is rather a starting point, since the ideology of liberal democracy is far less prescriptive than the others we have examined – it proposes a certain kind of container for society, but not its contents. Depending on their broader cultures, institutional histories, styles of governance and many other factors, liberal democracies differ in how they provide psychologically for their citizens – compare the US with Scandinavian countries, for example. In particular the extent to which they address the core needs for safety and dignity, and how they do so, will vary.

THE APPEAL OF VICTIMHOOD

There is a long-standing debate amongst psychologists and social scientists about whether aggression and destructiveness are an in-built part of human nature or the product of adverse experiences – deprivation, frustration, separation and so on. Psychoanalytic psychology has its own version of this debate, and its own methods (such as the close observation of very young babies) for gathering evidence relevant to it. Interesting though it is, we won't be looking into this debate in this book, for two reasons. One is that whatever its original source, aggression is present in the human infant from very early on, as psychoanalytic observational work has shown, so for the purposes of political psychology we must accept its ubiquitous presence in human affairs and proceed from there, rather than ponder on whether we have fallen from a condition of primal innocence. The second is that the intensity and quality of destructiveness in individuals varies hugely in ways that are clearly related to cultural and political conditions, so the most important task is for us to understand the specific social drivers of the most damaging forms of aggression if we are to improve the management of conflicts.

Nonetheless, there is reason to suggest that, primally innocent or not, we all carry an internal conviction of our own innocence. This can have been generated in experiences where we were actually the recipients of some hurtful action by another, but more fundamentally is an intrinsic quality of narcissistic experience. Acquiring the capacity to acknowledge guilt is a key element in the developmental process of growing out of the narcissistic defence. Within the bubble of narcissistic omnipotence, the reality of another self who is capable of suffering is at most faintly recognised, and so the question of whether you have hurt another does not really arise. So at all those frequent times when a state of mind might be heavily influenced by its narcissistic underbelly, there may be a surge of belief in one's innocence. Hence we can all potentially claim 'I am innocent!' with an element of subjective truth attached to it. Once, we were all innocent, though not as in the idealised childhood of purity.

This account of the latent plausibility and urgency with which we might claim innocence can help to understand the prominence and potency we have seen in many ideologies of the theme of victimhood. The Muslim as the global victim, the oppressed proletariat of Marxism, the 'left behind' enthusiasts for certain types of populist rhetoric, the neglected 'people' as the hero of all populisms, are all defined by their positions as innocents suffering from others' bad doings. The importance of victimhood, and our surprising attachment to it, is a major factor in the generation of conflict. Moreover, in the dynamic of competitive victimhood, when opposing sides each claim to be the greater victim in order to attract support from neutrals, and to convince themselves of their case, they become more entrenched in indignant aversion to negotiation and compromise.

5

PROSPECTS

If the current state of global politics is viewed with a psychological eye, it seems no better – perhaps worse – than when surveyed from more usual standpoints, from which we see failed and failing states, environmental crises, burgeoning terror, rising authoritarianism and so on. We have seen in previous chapters how some basic elements of human nature lie within the recurrent tragedies of oppressive rule and violent conflict, and how they complicate all efforts to move towards better societies. At the risk of disheartening the reader, we will move towards a conclusion by flagging up some major issues in the current political landscape which we have not discussed so far but each of which shows again the importance of our inner worlds in shaping political developments.

ENVIRONMENTAL CATASTROPHE

There is widespread denial about climate change. This is not the denial of the climate change deniers, who are relatively few in number; rather it is the attitude of the many who do not dispute there could be a problem but turn away from it or distract themselves elsewhere. This is not outright cognitive denial, but a denial, through one's behaviour, of the scale or urgency of the problem. Since climate change, and other environmental problems, pose threats to our physical home in the universe, and to our food supplies, it would be reasonable to assume that we will have stabs of deep anxiety about the potential losses involved. We project powerful images of fertility, strength and generational renewal into the natural world, and then consume those images ('reintroject' them, in the language of psychoanalysis) to support our confidence in the world as able to support us. Visions of damage and contamination across the whole world environment, and of wild and unpredictable weather, can dissolve the sense of security which we gain from the constancy of landscapes and oceans, and the routines of seasons and harvests. Pictures of melting ice floes and plastic-infested waters present us with damaged objects, for whose impending destruction we are responsible. And the subsequent guilt is about a *planetary* catastrophe; climate change activists are, perhaps inevitably, in the business of promoting apocalyptic scenarios.[1]

For some people there is an appeal in contemplating the drama of apocalypse, but most of us just want to turn away, towards something more hopeful. This is a matter of unconscious as well as conscious anxiety. Psychoanalysis tells us of very primitive, *catastrophic* fears of dying or disintegrating which can beset the baby in its helplessness, and which we continue to carry inside us unconsciously throughout life. Scenarios of threatened catastrophe can reactivate these primitive fears, feeding a hidden, internal resistance to confronting the threat as it exists in the external world. So our denial is not only at the level of a conscious reluctance to change our pleasurable and easy habits of consumption, in the service of which we deliberately marginalise our awareness of how bad the problem is, and allow ourselves to think that it may turn out to be not so bad. There is also an unconscious resonance to the prospect of disaster which reinforces our avoidance. We may adjust our behaviours a little (e.g. we recycle or try to shop responsibly), but environmental issues remain on the edges of most political contestation.

FAKE NEWS

Our political cultures are awash with suspicion of, and often con-
tempt for, those involved in politics. There is a broad cultural context
for this in the decline of deference, a process which has been going
on at least since the 1960s era of protest and counter-culture. So
this is not a recent development; by the 1990s a cynical outlook on
politics was established amongst many journalists and reflected in
the tone of their coverage in the mainstream media. But this century
has seen the negativity about politics become much wider and more
emphatic, not least because, in an ironic twist, the political media
themselves have become objects of deep suspicion. The concept of
'fake news' brings a new level of threat to democratic politics because
it attacks the legitimacy not of particular politicians or policies, but
of the whole public sphere of debate and deliberation, leaving people
free to withdraw from argument with anyone they disagree with,
and to ignore any critical scrutiny of their actions. In the age of the
web and social media, falsities can obviously proliferate freely, and
pose a major problem for democratic deliberation by confusing and
misleading us. But the even greater threat probably comes from the
accusations of falsity made in order to *close down* debate and inquiry,
in effect to close down politics.

While there are many examples of politicians who have acted in
ways that deserve public opprobrium, and of mendacious journalists,
something further is needed to push people into the incoherence
of the radically anti-political politics which have emerged in recent
years. It is as if we have become collectively unable to trust, an
attitude which if it gained sway over the economic, transactional
sphere of life would bring most things to a halt. It may yet do so
in the political sphere. How do we understand this crisis of trust?
Drawing on the approach taken in this book, we would assume that
there is always some form of internal driver alongside the external
ones. As many commentators have suggested, cynicism and hostility
towards elites is partly grounded in feelings of abandonment and

betrayal. On some occasions, such feelings may be fully understood and justified as responses to actual events and situations. On others, as we noted in Chapter 2, we have to ask whether some residue of fears and resentments from early development is at work. In any case, the full extent and implications of the collapse of trust are not yet clear, and the process is ongoing.

THE GROWTH FIXATION

In wealthier parts of the world, political publics seem to be mes-merised by the 'economy' and particularly by economic 'growth'. Most mainstream political discourse takes growth to be axiomatically good and necessary, such that there is a serious problem if it does not occur at a vigorous rate. Headlines that say economic indicators are 'flatlining' worry governments. Of course, the vision of human civilisation proceeding to ever-greater abundance is attractive, and economic growth is important, but strategies for the enrichment of human societies should not be guided by a purely quantitative index which does not discriminate much between different areas of growth, and so lacks any kind of moral compass. Moreover, many of the problems which, we are told, growth is going to enable us to solve could also be tackled by redistributive measures. Despite the increasing number of voices now calling for a basic re-evaluation of growth ideology, we seemingly continue to subscribe to a phantasy about the 'economy' as a huge force that surrounds us. It usually evades our attempts to control it, and it demands that we pacify and please it. If we can do its bidding, it grows and 'booms', and is libidinally exciting and permissive. More often, it has an admonish-ing, oppressive superego identity, telling us we have done wrong, we have hurt it, and now we must suffer so that it can recover and grow again. At all times, we are being asked to stay in an anxious and compliant role in relation to the 'economy', as one might with a demanding and volatile parent.

GROWING INEQUALITIES

Finally, there is the problem of growing inequality, focussed on in recent years by, amongst many others, the geographer Danny Dorling, the economist Thomas Piketty and the epidemiologists Richard Wilkinson and Kate Pickett. The general emphasis in this book has been away from economic issues, towards questions of leader-follower relations, cultural identity and ideological mindset. 'Economistic' approaches to politics have been unfavourably compared here with psychosocial ones, alongside which they seem simplistic and rationalistic. So it may seem surprising that we should end on the topic of socio-economic inequality.

In discussing how the psychological defences of narcissism, splitting, projection and so on can shape our experience of politics, we noted the origins of these defences in experiences of unsafety and humiliation. If it were possible to make early and skilled interventions into the family lives of all babies and young children whose emotional development was at risk, our politics, and societies as a whole, might look a lot brighter. Hopefully, access to sophisticated psychotherapeutic help will increase across the world, with benefits to individuals and their communities in all areas of life, and this ought to be a strategic political priority. But the problems we have been describing in this book, though located in the minds of individuals, need addressing at systemic and primary level; they are too endemic to be dealt with otherwise. The most fundamental primary level is that of culture, and how cultural values shape parenting and family life. While cultures are always changing, changing them by design in specific directions is likely to be a slow and uncertain process. However, some cultural values can be strongly influenced by social arrangements, and some of those can be directly changed through political action.

Specifically, economic inequality can be changed through politics, and there are reasons to think that reducing inequality would impact on the socio-cultural life of a society in ways that would change the values and the experiences of people in that society. These changes could lead on to experiences of enhanced safety and dignity, and the political benefits which would flow from that. To illustrate this, we will take a very brief look at the influential work of Wilkinson and Pickett (2009), which unlike most of the other studies and sources we have considered is a piece of number-crunching, mainstream social science. It is of particular interest though because of the direct connections they make between economic inequality, culture and psychology.

Common sense would lead us to think that all kinds of problems are worse in poor societies than in wealthy ones, that the overall wealth of a nation is the most fundamental factor in determining the quality of life and contentment it can offer its citizens. Basic measures of societal well-being such as life expectancy and the self-reported happiness of the population are lowest in the poorest societies. But once basic levels of material wealth are achieved, the links between wealth and welfare disappear, and another piece of everyday wisdom takes over: money can't buy happiness, nor even health. The affluence of the developed world sometimes seems to be a curse rather than a blessing. So instead of comparing nations in terms of their overall wealth, Wilkinson and Pickett approached the question of wealth and well-being from a different angle. They took a sample of richer countries, and compared them according to the distribution of wealth within each nation.

Nations can be ranked using various formulae in terms of how unequal they are on the dimensions of personal and household income. Using one of these formulae, Wilkinson and Pickett found many strong relationships between inequality and indices of social and health problems. Life expectancy, infant mortality, the incidence of mental illness, drug use, educational performance – all were significantly worse in more unequal societies, no matter how wealthy they were. This relationship found at the international level between inequality and problems also appeared when the researchers compared states within the US.

So how can inequality be more important than absolute levels of wealth in determining the well-being of a nation? Wilkinson and Pickett are not psychologists, but found that to explain their findings, it was necessary to take a psychological turn. They drew on research in the field of health psychology, from which they took the concept of 'social-evaluative threats'. This refers to comparisons of the self with others in which there is a risk of negative evaluation, that is of feeling that one's self or one's life is not as good as others'. These are potent health-damaging stressors. In more unequal societies there will be more opportunities for people to make invidious comparisons between themselves and others, and to feel that others are more secure, more respected, more happy and so on. This is the basis of the link between inequality on the one hand and health and social problems on the other. Crucially, those in the upper strata will be affected as much as those lower down the income scale. This is an area for further research, but Wilkinson and Pickett suggest that more unequal societies are likely to be more competitive, and to produce higher levels of insecurity about status for everyone. Also, as the psychoanalytic theory of groups would tell us, if disturbing feelings of insecurity or humiliation are strongly felt amongst some members of society, this will affect all. Those feelings can be projected and shared widely, while the sense of being in a divided and unjust society will seriously reduce the potentially containing influence which societal membership, through the sense of belonging, can have on all our anxieties.

They had also noted an apparent paradox in the survey data that they had reviewed when exploring health trends. People often report that stress levels of various kinds are increasing, yet another trend in the data indicated that levels of self-esteem are rising. Surely under greater stress, people will feel less good about themselves? This can be explained, however, as Wilkinson and Pickett noted, by seeing the measures of self-esteem as a reflection of an increasing recourse to a narcissistic defence, in the face of intensifying social-evaluative threats.

Their hypothesis and their data offer clear support for the ideas advanced in this book about the key role, in shaping political outlooks and actions, of the safety and dignity principles, narcissistic defences and other regressive aspects of psychological functioning we outlined in Chapter 1. So, at the end of a book on the psychology of politics, in which the main argument has been for more attention to be paid to the power of our minds and characters to shape our politics, we come to the hopeful possibility that pursuing a particular political agenda and focussing on socio-economic inequality might be one contribution to shaping our minds, and to help build up our emotional capital (which feeds back into politics). We have focussed on the core psychological problems of unsafety and humiliation, and how these play out in our relations to leaders, in our national identities, and in our views about how society should be organised (our ideologies). It is likely that gross social inequalities are a significant source of these problems, which can have very toxic effects when mobilised in politics, whether in response to a leader's malignant charisma, in defensive-aggressive collective identities, in the brutalities of terrorism, or in other ways. Against these toxins, we should note that there are countervailing emotional resources which human cultures around the globe spontaneously reproduce in their children, to varying degrees – the capacities to feel safe, to trust, to tolerate humiliation, and to contain anxiety, guilt and grief.

FURTHER READING

Bar-Tal, D. (2013) *Intractable Conflicts. Socio-Psychological Foundations and Dynamics.* Cambridge: Cambridge University Press. Influential theory of conflict, based in social psychology not psychoanalysis but converges with Volkan's ideas.

Bowlby, J. (1988) *A Secure Base.* Abingdon: Routledge, revised edn., 2005. Key papers by Bowlby on attachment theory and its applications.

Erikson, E. (1950) *Childhood and Society.* Harmondsworth: Penguin, revised edn., 1965. Erikson's classical psychosocial text; includes an essay on Hitler's childhood.

Frank, J. (2012) *Obama on the Couch: Inside the Mind of the President.* New York: Free Press. One of Frank's insightful series of psychoanalytic studies of presidents.

Freud, S. (1921) Group psychology and the analysis of the ego. In *Penguin Freud Library,Vol. 12: Civilization, Society and Religion.* Harmondsworth: Penguin, revised edn., 1991. A good place to start reading original Freud.

Fromm, E. (1949) *Man for Himself.* London: Ark, revised edn., 1986. Old-fashioned in title and to some extent in content, but Fromm's work on 'social character' is still well worth reading.

Greenfeld, L. (2016) *Advanced Introduction to Nationalism.* Cheltenham: Edward Elgar. Makes the case for the link between national identity and dignity.

Guntrip, H. (1971) *Psychoanalytic Theory, Therapy and the Self.* London: Karnac, revised edn., 1977. Explains the major differences between classical Freudian theory and the 'object-relations' development of psychoanalysis.

Hoggett, P. (2009) *Politics, Identity and Emotion*. Boulder, CO: Paradigm. An exploration in more scholarly detail of many of the key issues in this book and others.

Lindholm, C. (1990) *Charisma*. Oxford: Blackwell. An integration of sociological and psychoanalytic thinking about charisma, with case studies.

Lindner, E. (2006) *Making Enemies: Humiliation and International Conflict*. Westport, CT: Praeger Publishers. One of the few psychological studies which puts dignity/humiliation at the centre of its theory.

Mintchev, N. & Hinshelwood, R.D. (2017) *The Feeling of Certainty: Psychosocial Perspectives on Identity and Difference*. Cham, Switzerland: Palgrave. Psychoanalytic essays on the psychic bases of prejudice, dogma and fundamentalism.

Mitchell, J., ed. (1986) *The Selected Melanie Klein*. Harmondsworth: Penguin. A collection of many key readings in the Kleinian development of Freud.

Richards, B. (2007) *Emotional Governance: Politics, Media and Terror*. Basingstoke: Palgrave Macmillan. Offers a framework for understanding public feeling, with responses to terror as a case study.

Rustin, M. (1991) *The Good Society and the Inner World*. London: Verso. Essays on Kleinian psychoanalysis, politics and philosophy by a leading psychosocial thinker.

Volkan, V. (2004) *Blind Trust: Large Groups and their Leaders in Times of Crisis and Terror*. Charlottesville, VA: Pitchstone Publishing. Volkan's theory of large group dynamics, with many major case studies.

Volkan, V., Itzkowitz, N. & Dod, A. (1997) *Richard Nixon: A Psychobiography*. New York: Columbia University Press. Another demonstration of how psychoanalytic psychobiography can help make sense of individual leadership.

Winnicott, D. (1986) *Home Is Where We Start From: Essays by a Psychoanalyst*. Harmondsworth: Penguin. Very readable and wide-ranging essays by a key figure in post-Freudian psychoanalysis.

Yates, C. (2015) *The Play of Political Culture, Emotion and Identity*. Basingstoke: Palgrave Macmillan. Links psychoanalysis with cultural studies in the analysis of electoral politics.